THE
EVOLUTION
OF LOVE

The Kiss by Rodin

THE EVOLUTION OF LOVE

ADA LAMPERT

Human Evolution, Behavior, and Intelligence
Seymour W. Itzkoff, Series Editor

Westport, Connecticut
London

Library of Congress Cataloging-in-Publication Data

Lampert, Ada.
    [Evolutsyah shel ha-ahavah. English]
    The evolution of love / Ada Lampert.
        p. cm.—(Human evolution, behavior, and intelligence, ISSN
    1063–2158)
    Includes bibliographical references and index.
    ISBN 0–275–95907–4 (alk. paper)
    1. Love. 2. Love—Physiological aspects. 3. Behavior evolution.
    I. Title. II. Series.
    BF575.L8L26513   1997
    155.7—dc21   97–11073

British Library Cataloguing in Publication Data is available.

Library of Congress Catalog Card Number: 97–11073
ISBN: 0–275–95907–4
ISSN: 1063–2158

First published in 1997

Praeger Publishers, 88 Post Road West, Westport, CT 06881
An imprint of Greenwood Publishing Group, Inc.

Printed in the United States of America

∞™

The paper used in this book complies with the
Permanent Paper Standard issued by the National
Information Standards Organization (Z39.48–1984).

10 9 8 7 6 5 4 3 2

To my daughter, Yael

CONTENTS

FIGURES

INTRODUCTION

The theory of evolution has perhaps become the strongest and most central tool of thought for those struggling to explain the world. Traditionally, this theory has been employed by biologists who explain fauna and flora, and are slightly apprehensive about explaining humans. In recent years, the boundaries of this tradition have been breaking down, and those whose interests lie in the human sciences—sociologists, anthropologists, historians, economists, philosophers, physicians, geneticists, and psychologists—have discovered the greatness of the evolution theory and want to make use of it. The first obstacle that hinders the study of humans as a result of natural selection processes is the concept of the soul. People accept the description of the evolution of our body with relative ease. It is easy to understand that feet were selected for their ability to bear us, and hands for their ability to bear booty. But love is "spiritual"; it is not to be constrained in the dryness and simplicity of biology, but is to be left floating ethereal, innocent of any material reality.

In his genius, Darwin understood a hundred and fifty years ago that mental characteristics are hereditary and therefore subject to the laws of natural selection, in the same way that physical traits are. Through wise observation of his own children's development, he remarked on fears that were not the result of any experience, but appeared in all children at the same age. It can, therefore, be concluded that these fears are hereditary. He also noticed that, starting at the age of two, his sons found the talent and inclination to throw objects at a target, whereas his daughters did not. Again he asked himself whether the heredity of behavioral inclinations in boys should be considered to be different from that in girls. Darwin viewed his children's development of verbal abilities in their first year as a sort of repetition of the evolution of language, from monkeys who make do with cries and sounds to the very precise articulation of humans.

Since the very beginnings of this psychological biology, brain, nervous system, and hormone research, though still in its infancy, has produced such abundant findings that it is easier for us to view love, the ability to love, and the need to be loved as products of natural selection processes. These processes began with the lower mammals and reached their peak in humans.

For the amateur audience the natural selection principle claims that if a certain characteristic has been selected, then it must be good. We have to beware of this trap, which might be called "the Little Red Riding Hood trap." Little Red Riding Hood asks: "Grandmother, why do you have such big eyes?" and Grandmother answers: "The better to see you with." And again Little Red Riding Hood asks: "Grandmother, why do you have such big ears?" and is answered: "The better to hear you with." According to superfine evolution theory, however, no trait was selected in order to serve a purpose. Rather, it was selected only after it accidentally appeared, without purpose, and was found to serve the ability to reproduce offspring.

Thinking that grandmother has big eyes in order to see will also cause us to believe that someone was busy planning the solution to grandmother's needs even before she was created: God, a creator, a supreme power, someone. Evolution theory forgoes this belief, and in so doing also forgoes the illusion of advance planning and of optimal solutions. The solutions, that is, our traits, are not optimal but are reasonable. If they were optimal, we might have had wings with which to hover over traffic jams. But feet are a reasonable solution to mobility problems, and to this day they are the mobility organ that was selected in us—not in order to, but because of, post-factum. Even the degree of "reasonability" can change, when the conditions under which it operates change. Hunger, the ability to detect, obtain, swallow and digest food, as much as the great pleasure derived from this process were selected after they were found to serve purposes of survival. In a society where food is abundant, however, all these urges work overtime, excessively and harmfully. And if you wish to survive, you must keep yourself from overeating. Voracity, which was no doubt selected by natural selection processes in difficult ancient times, has become a negative drive in modern affluent society.

Similarly, the behavior that produces offspring was selected with a strong urge towards and then satisfaction at its implementation. A creature does not have to "want" to reproduce; it is enough for it to feel the urge and pleasure from the sexual act. Evolution will carry on from there. Modern, self-conscious man is keenly aware of the possibility of seeking sexual pleasure while blocking its original function—reproduction. Our sexuality has become separated from the evolutionary context in which it was selected. A wise discussion of human behavior would call for much more complicated thought, rather than the oversimplified claim that what was selected is "good." The opposite simplicity—that whatever does not produce offspring was not selected—is just as shallow. A pair of lovers can decide that they prefer leisure and a career to dealing with annoying children, and they are still a product of evolution, which selects traits for reproduction. It selected sexual desire in this couple, and that was enough. Intelligence, with all its enormous evolutionary advantages, was selected later, but from the moment it existed it could invent contraceptives.

Our selected traits are made of matter—genes, hormones, the nervous system, the brain—and they are durable and eager to express themselves. They "aspire to self-realization," to act. This aspiration could be autonomous, and self-realization could exceed its original context. As our talent to enjoy sex is already built in, it can be accomplished in order to strengthen the relationship between two people, to dominate each other, to derive pleasure, or even to become addicted to. All these might run free until they cause damage to success in the evolutionary sense. The same goes for love.

The attempt to explain love as an evolutionary process will benefit if it is conducted with extreme care. In this text, we shall employ the power of natural selection theory, base our arguments on as many research findings as possible, and suggest skeptic conclusions.

1

LOVE IS MATTER

One of the most perplexing questions people ask themselves is, "What was before?" What was before humans, and what was before life? What was there before earth was formed, and what existed before the world was created? We should better assume that we will never find an answer, religious or scientific, after which we will never again hope to plague ourselves with the question "What was before that?" This backtracking in time can never end.

But whoever wants to tell the story of the world anyway can choose a point in time at which to begin. Nowadays, it is easy to start with "Big Bang," that singular event from which the universe, as we know it, was created. A dense mass of matter, altogether smaller than the eye can see, suddenly, furiously exploded, and its particles have been scattering all over from that moment onward for the past 15 billion years. These particles are our world and they are us. In the process of being scattered, from the center outward, they "behave," meet each other, get acquainted and move on together, or push each other, or run away from each other. When they combine, they become a new substance, more complex than the elementary particle. When a number of groups combine into a community, a new and even more complex substance is formed, which holds internal relationships: some are trapped together, others circle around them, and others yet gather in the center or at the edges. Thus is "matter" created: atom, molecule, earth, water, sky, planet, star, sun, moon, galaxy—all are products of the behavior of the elementary particles in their flight from the center outward.

Our universe, and everything in it, is constructed of these elementary building blocks, which when combined into a complex form over a long enough period of time create a durable entity. As long as these particles have momentum, they are restless and continue to act—pushing and running, combining and separating, creating new forms and ceasing to exist in others. The momentum of these particles and their mutual influence are also the meaning behind concepts, which traditionally fog our understanding: energy, radiation, conduction, temperature, gravity—are all acting particles. In the old world of concepts, "stone" was concrete matter, whereas "light" was an abstract phenomenon. In the brave new world of concepts, light is a swift flow of elementary particles—photons. This is a big stone, and these are fast little stones, a shower of tiny stones rained down upon us by the sun.

Whoever is prepared to accept this physicist's description of our world, and is not willing to add a belief in the existence of a mysterious force outside this created universe, necessarily also accepts the premise, and the challenge to explain it, that life itself, its evolution, its rich variety of form, the ever increasing complexity of structure and behavior—are all nothing but wondrous and supreme expressions of the behavior of the elementary particles. Life itself is nothing but matter. For there is nothing but the particles of the Big Bang in this space.

Just as the atom was created, and the molecule and earth and the water above it, so life appeared governed by the same processes and the same laws, constituting elementary particles in a stable, close-knit group. The living molecule appeared 4 billion years ago, and to this day, it is one and the same—so-called DNA (deoxyribonucleic acid). Life, as far as we know, appeared only once, and the entire rich variety of living forms is the metamorphosis, the evolution, of this molecule. How does life differ from inanimate matter? By the inner structure of the molecule, a structure that has far-reaching implications. The uniqueness of this molecular structure, as opposed to any other molecule, lies in the fact that its borders are made of meticulous connoisseurs, also close-knit groups of particles, who inspect potential partners and choose only those whose addition to their group will recreate or replicate themselves. Replication of the existing molecular structure by the joining together of identical raw materials, wandering around in a nearby space, is the very essence of the phenomenon called life. The DNA molecule is "alive" because it replicates itself and thus creates new life, reproducing offspring.

From the moment life first appeared, it has been carrying on from generation to generation by means of replication. This process serves the live molecule in two ways: it creates offspring just like itself, and it creates organs to serve it. The cell and the cell nucleus, organelles within the cell, groups of cells, and complete physiological systems in which the original DNA is replicated, but each has a different function—respiration, blood, digestion, procreation, sensation, movement, are all organs in the service of the live molecule. Replication means copying, and a reliable copy is the cornerstone to life. But endless production series call for a certain number of mistakes, namely mutations, and these create new life forms over and over again. This is what evolution means.

The process of evolution has been going on like this for the past 4 billion years. The initial molecule, DNA, amasses mutations for their ability to improve the replication process under its given environmental conditions, and constantly produces new structures, traits, and behavior. The mutations are amassed after they have been examined in the face of reality. That which grows an organ or a type of behavior, and that which will aid in the replication process, is selected and gathered into the initial DNA. This is the natural selection process that designs the life changes from generation to generation and that constantly measures the DNA molecule's ability to reproduce itself. Natural selection selects advantages that either directly or indirectly will help to produce offspring. It selected the tail for its advantage in cruising, it selected the feet for their advantage in walking, it selected the eyes for their advantage in perceiving the world, it selected fear for its advantage in bewaring of enemies, and it selected love for its advantage in mutual relationships.

Love is a product of evolution, which has (very successfully) passed the test of natural selection; it consists of the particles of the Big Bang and functions among them. In 1970, the prestigious journal *Nature* published a study that an anonymous investigator conducted with himself as subject. For the sake of his scientific work, Anonymous stayed on a lonely island, leaving it only every few weeks to meet his wife. Being bored and clever, Anonymous gathered the bristles of his beard when he shaved every morning, placed them carefully on the scales, and wrote down their weight. Within a few months, he discovered a recurring regularity in the recorded results: the closer his vacation approached, the more sexual fantasies concerning his wife he had. And the more sexual fantasies he had, the heavier became the beard bristles he weighed. The male hormone testosterone plays a part in the two events: its level rises with sexual fantasies, and it encourages beard growth. When Anonymous imagined sexual scenes, his brain buzzed with molecular events: various matter (Big Bang particles) are on the move within neural cells, pushing other matter, cohering and separating, so that "thought" rises to his conscious. These same particles pushed and were pushed into Anonymous's testicles and activated DNA sections, genes, which are required to increase testosterone production; testosterone is also matter, which in turn pushes and is pushed to the cheeks to increase beard growth. This is a classic scenario of complex life: sexual fantasies, which are matter, grow the beard, which is matter, as part of the love connection, between a man and woman, which is entirely matter.

The initial live matter was around many years before the matter of love. Love is a new phenomenon and is at its peak in humans. This book intends to tell the story of the evolution of love. How and why did the mutations, which prepare live matter to love, come to be selected by right and become a central and important part of the human's genetic equipment? Which mutations combined with the ancient DNA and made the living creature a loving creature?

In order for the living body to produce and use testosterone, the DNA molecule must include genes whose replication will enable testosterone production. For instance, genes for enzymes that can synthesize steroid hormones from the cholesterol we consume. When the hormone is produced, flows in the bloodstream, and reaches its destination, it stimulates male activity, builds male body and brain structures, and generates male behavior—which are beneficial to the replication process. The genes, which can produce testosterone, were therefore selected by means of natural selection.

DNA sections, genes, which when replicated create the matter of love, are numerous and have a wide variety of functions. They dictate the production of hormones. They dictate the production of the neural pathways that evoke arousal, excitement, joy, anxiety, and sadness. They dictate the structure and functioning of brain structures, which know how to receive, decipher, make decisions, and give instructions about loving behavior. They also dictate the sensitivity of the skin (by means of receptors, which are made up of Big Bang particles, of course) to a stroke and to a warm hand (which again, of course, is made up of particles that have coalesced into a stable form), and the sensitivity of the ear to warm words.

These and many others make up a package of matter, which orchestrates the "talent" to love. A closely similar package orchestrates the "thirst" to be loved. Both packages are interwoven in the physiological fabric, to the point of interdependence among the warfare, satisfaction, and pleasure one feels with the existence of the "right condition" according to evolution: the presence of love. The opposite is also true. Separation, the loss of love, its amputation, and its lack activate a package of neural, cerebral, hormonal matter that we call yearning. When Anonymous went on his mission and left his loving wife alone, she could have (parallel to weighing of the beard) measured the increase of the hormone prolactin in her blood. Prolactin, as its name suggests, is the milk-producing hormone. The genes responsible for its production were selected for the contribution of milk to procreation. But breast-feeding is concerned with proximity and the desire to be close, mother to child. Therefore, an additional task was selected for prolactin, and it activates yearning in our brains and then in the rest of our bodies, seeking the proximity of the loved one. Separation increases prolactin, so that it in turn hurries to cancel the separation and return the lovers to each other's arms.

In a study conducted in 1986 on 117 breast-cancer patients in Israel, I found that 65% of them experienced difficult separations from their parents in childhood, as opposed to 18% of separations in a control group of healthy women and as 36% of separations in a control group of women with other types of cancer (see Figure 1). Why would a girl who experienced a difficult separation risk breast cancer of all things? Because the same hormone that fights separations is also busy producing milk, and when it increases in order to cope with the lack of love, it activates the milk glands in vain. At times, this could go so far as to create growths.

Anonymous's wife may not have known about the dangers of yearning, but she certainly knew that she yearned. An increased level of prolactin can be detected in many animals when they experience separation. The knowledge of and the ability to report the feeling of yearning are unique to humans. But we should not be misled by this uniqueness. Awareness is but another stable form

Figure 1
Breast Cancer and Childhood Separations

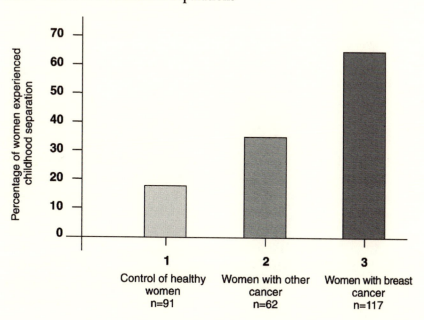

of Big Bang particles, which was selected to become a wondrous human talent. It also is a package of neural pathways that conduct matter, pushing and being pushed, to the point where "awareness" emerges and is even expressed in words. Every word is a bustling dynamics of scores of elementary particles in infinitely complex structures.

Genes are made of matter and are selected for their ability to generate a cascade of material processes, just like a snowball that generates a wide-scale snow avalanche: the construction of cells, tissues, organs, a network of neurons that evoke messages, supreme command centers in the brain, highly complex activities of supervision, control, and processing—up to the point of creating feelings, thoughts, words, and conscience. All these are the end results of the basic momentum of our world, as well as of the simple basic trait of a DNA molecule—replication.

Even if we feel that love is sublime, celestial, and transcendental, we are greatly obligated to the wonders of the matter, which originated in the Big Bang.

2

GENES FOR LOVE

Students of evolution, especially those who study the evolution of love, are faced with a not so easy dilemma of values. Modern Western philosophy glorifies science and the scientific way of reaching conclusions, based on the hard facts of quantification, measurement, and microscopic viewing. But the stories of evolution are not always of the kind that can be placed under a microscope, especially not those concerning the evolution of the special human traits that enable us to love. These have not left behind fossils in some geological strata. And yet, these are the very questions we so urgently want to ask and to find the answers to. Do we have the right?

The same right we take when we suggest an evolutionary explanation of a physical characteristic, such as an organ, a tail, an eye, or an ear, is valid when we try to find the evolutionary explanation of feeling, behavior, the brain, and even consciousness and love. The task is difficult, but those who adhere only to what can be placed under a microscope are falling into the same trap as does the drunk who searches for his lost key under the street lamp. If the key is there, that is all well and good. But there is a big chance that the key is elsewhere, somewhere in the dark space surrounding the lamp, and the drunk will do better to search there as well. Quite probably, the keys to many evolutionary stories are in the still dark spaces, where we ought to try and look, although we might at times find ourselves telling tales that include quite a bit of speculation. The same is true about the evolution of love. Love is one of the most intense, dramatic, powerful experiences known to humans. It is sometimes perceived as stronger than life itself. "Love is as fierce as death" says the Song of Songs, "Omnia Vincit Amor." Our thirst for love is so intense that it seems as if our entire lives are about what happens to us during the restless pursuit of love. That is why we wish so much to discover the story of its evolution.

In discussing the evolution of love, we are obliged to make two assumptions. The first states that the talent to love and to be loved, as well as the need to seek love, is part of human genetic equipment and is passed on from parents to children via heredity. The second states that this talent appeared somewhere along the lines of life on earth and has been undergoing changes since then by natural selection. These changes are what brought love in humans to such intensity.

If love was indeed selected by natural selection processes, it was selected according to the universal criterion of evolution: contribution to the reproduction of offspring. The essence of natural selection is that it selects those traits, which have an advantage in the process of reproduction. We must, therefore, look for the advantages of the talent to love adjacent to the giving birth to and the raising of children. Indeed, the two major loves that we experience are sexual love and parental love—the love that brings children into the world and the love that raises them.

Pure sexuality, as opposed to love, is a genetic-determined phenomenon billions of years old and is shared by many creatures, who are much older than we in the evolutionary sense and to whom we do not tend to apply the talent to love. When a male lizard mates with a female, we view it as a sexual act, not one of love. But natural selection, in its own way, grooms this start over the generations to higher and higher complexities, to better and better perfection, and adds increasingly more mechanisms to initial sexuality, which turn the sexual process into something more precise, fine-tuned, and thus more successful. Love is the tool that assists us to correctly select a mate, to calibrate and gently adjust the process of sexual selection. Children are not reproduced with just anyone, but with someone with whom the prospect of success is the highest.

Sexual love is an evolutionary-designed tool that guides our selection of a mate. How does it do it? The judgment process involved in whom one falls in love with is based on a large number of criteria. Not all are known, of course, and we will not go into all of those that are known. We will simply deal with two of them, namely, point and counterpoint. The first is the mechanism that guides us to fall in love with a person who is genetically similar to ourselves. The second, on the contrary, is the mechanism that distances us from those who are genetically too similar to ourselves. Both criteria design the process of falling in love as a selection of one who has optimal genetic similarity to ourselves.

How does genetic similarity contribute to our success in reproducing offspring? Let's imagine Mr. So-and-So falling in love with a cow. They might make a very nice couple, experiencing lots of peace and quiet, warmth and harmony. They would never quarrel, and their refrigerator would always be full of dairy products. But they would no doubt lack one thing—children. This nice couple is doomed to childlessness because of the genetic distance between the father's contribution and the mother's contribution, which denies the means for DNA replication. There will, therefore, be no pregnancy, no fetus, no birth.

Falling in love with a gorilla is on the right track, but the genetic distance is still to great. But a chimpanzee, surprisingly enough, is a real possibility. The genetic distance between humans and chimpanzees is less than 2%. Since 98% of genetic matter in chimpanzees and humans is identical, reproduction is quite probable. However, children are not the final end; they are but the means. The final end is grandchildren, and this is where difficult problems will arise. If we try to imagine a child born to a human and a chimpanzee, we can easily guess that it would be neither good-looking nor very smart, and it is doubtful whether anyone would choose it as a mate. So, the dynasty would come to its end before any grandchildren would be born. It is, therefore, better for a man to fall in love with a woman, and of all women he will select the one most similar to himself, even within the same town and the same community.

An ever lengthening list of studies has found advantages in mates with great similarities. For instance, the higher the genetic similarity is, the higher fertility rates will be. Fewer abortions and healthier children will follow. In addition, the levels of altruism and mutual assistance within the family are higher, harmony and stability in the couple's life are better, and their marriage satisfaction is greater. No one probes and measures genetic similarity before they fall in love, and if evolution has indeed selected a mechanism that attracts us to similar mates, then it was made an unconscious process, which acts without our knowledge. Researchers of love cannot ask those who fall in love whether they felt the genetic similarity, when they first met the object of their love. If so, how can we study this unconscious inclination?

Philip Rushton, a Canadian professor of psychology, found a genuine way to study this unconscious inclination. He studied about a thousand files of paternity suits in each of which a woman, who had given birth sued the courts to pronounce the man with whom she had sex as the baby's father. The courts settle such cases by genetic testing. If a high genetic similarity is found between the father and the offspring, he is pronounced the father. Rushton examined these cases for a different question: namely, to which degree are the man and woman genetically similar? He, indeed, found that a man and a woman who had a sexual relationship, and were therefore at least at the beginning of sexual love, were genetically more similar to each other than random couples, which the computer compiled from the same files. Generalization of Rushton's findings would permit us to assume that a couple in any community, neighborhood, town, or village are more similar to each other than to their next-door neighbors! Somehow, unconsciously, people detect genetic similarity in the other and feel sexually attracted.

If we were to take the search for genetic similarity to its extreme, a person would have to fall in love with his mother because she assuredly shares more than 50% of his genes. But if this were so, and everybody were to fall in love with their mothers, at least two new problems would arise. The first would be the increase of harmful recessive genes, which damage the offspring's fitness, add to diseases and disabilities, and certainly does not lead to evolutionary success. The second problem would be the reduction of the genetic variance pool, the job of which is to suggest new devices for future times of need. When Mom and Dad are very similar to each other, few genetic innovations can be found in their offspring. The first problem, harmful recessive genes, can be solved, at least in theory, by a process of eliminating selection; this has been achieved in some types of wheat, for instance. But the second problem has no easy solution. Variance is an essential requirement, mainly in large, complex creatures, as the prominent English biologist William Hamilton urged, because they are on a constant neck-to-neck "arms race" against viruses and germs, and a frequently renewed variety of antibodies is necessary. Living creatures can constantly replenish their immunization weapon reserves, as long as they replenish their genetic variance. Genes are the antibodies' producers and reduction of gene variance will serve the enemy.

For this reason, natural selection, always eager to succeed in reproducing offspring, had to find some mechanism to stop the drive for similarity and to enable a proper measure of variance. This is the origin of the strong incest taboo. There is a "Stop" sign on the continuum of genetic similarity, which leads from cow to mother. We do not rush to the very end of the continuum, but stop somewhere before the end. There is a "No Entry" sign in front of mothers and sisters. Indeed, most people observe this instruction, and not just humans. Mice, field voles, chimpanzees, Rhesus monkeys, Japanese monkeys, Japanese quail, Israeli babblers, and possibly other creatures not yet studied also observe it. Some plants like the almond-tree or the mountain delphinium are intelligent enough to distinguish relatives from nonrelatives and avoid too close kin pollen.

Which mechanism ensures the repudiation of incest? Now that we have spoken of falling in love as the mechanism that ensures our attraction to those similar to us, we must look for some mechanism that will stop us before we cross the threshold of incest. Such a mechanism apparently exists, and it is called negative imprinting. This term means that individuals with whom we spend the early years of our childhood are not sexually attractive to us because they are negatively imprinted on our brains. A good example of the relation between negative imprinting and retaining a varied and rich immune system can be found in mice.

Young mice imprint the scent of those who surround them in childhood, family members, of course, on their brains. In adulthood, searching for a mate, the mouse sniffs the prospective mate, and if the scent is familiar, it avoids copulation. The gene responsible for this smell is located in a chromosome right next to the important genetic complex of the immune system, the major histocompatibility complex (MHC). So, when the mouse recoils from a certain scent, it is, in fact, ensuring its offspring's renewal of their antibody system. Evolution loved it, and this avoidance was selected.

In humans, the influence of negative imprinting is apparent, in particular, when it is mistakenly applied to nonfamily. Let us look at two famous examples. In his Ph.D. dissertation in 1971, Joseph Shepher studied 2,679 marriages of kibbutz-born youngsters in Israel. In the kibbutz of the past, children spent their days and nights in a communal children's house rather than with their parents. As a result, children were much more exposed to their peers than to their family members. The mate-choice patterns of kibbutz youngsters show total avoidance of their own peers. In only 14 cases did both husband and wife belong to the same age group, and in only 5 out of these 14 cases did they grow up together before the age of six. Among these 5 couples, not even one couple had spent all the first six years of their lives together. In other words, kibbutz children who grew up together in early childhood do not tend to marry each other, although they are, of course, not prohibited from doing so.

The second example is from Taiwan, where it is customary to adopt children for later matchmaking purposes. A baby girl is given in adoption to the parents of a baby boy. In this way, the girl's parents save her upbringing costs, and the boy's parents save the high bride-price. Both grow up as siblings, and in time they are expected to marry. That is when troubles begin. They refuse, they evade, they run away. If they do obey, their matrimonial life is bitter, divorce rates are high, fertility is low (many of the children born are the fruits of adultery), and their sex life is not very satisfying.

In both the Taiwan and the Israeli kibbutz cases, the customs of bringing up children go beyond the normal case. The children are not so much surrounded by family members as by strangers. But the mechanism of negative imprinting works here too because it was selected and is inherited in every human genetic package. It was selected for the situation in which the child, in its early years, meets family members whom it will avoid. The kibbutz children's avoidance of each other and that of the Taiwanese matches are really mistaken and superfluous actions of negative imprinting. When everything is normal and children grow up with and around their parents, they are not attracted to them. They are negatively imprinted.

What, then, happened to Oedipus? Oedipus fell in love with his mother and married her, and Freud made him into a symbol of all children, doomed to fall in love with their mothers. But the Oedipus story points to the weakness of Freud's theory because Oedipus was taken away from his mother at birth and did not know her until he grew up. He met her when he was a young man and of all the beautiful, young maidens of Thebe he preferred his mother, possibly because of the falling-in-love mechanism, which seeks genetic similarity. The "No Entry" sign did not work for lack of negative imprinting, and this was lacking because Oedipus the child did not spend his childhood years with his mother.

As opposed to Freud's theory, according to which children extricate themselves from sexual attraction to their parents through fears of castration and loss, most children are free of the Oedipal complex to begin with, simply because they grow up among their family members and are negatively imprinted. Imprinting easily shapes the brains of very young children, whose brains are soft and impressionable, being like clay in the potter's hands. Negative imprinting concerning sexual attraction does indeed take place in the soft brains of children. The parents, on the other hand, have hardened brains, and imprinting does not happen easily there. Therefore, a parent might be attracted to his or her child. A great number of parents, mainly fathers, feel attraction toward their beautiful, adolescent daughters. Most fathers, however, avoid and protect their daughters and themselves. Some, like Freud, "project" the attraction they feel onto their daughters and call it an "Oedipal complex." And, alas, a few force themselves on their daughters. Children are free of sexual attraction to their parents, but love is, of course, much more than merely sex, and children love their parents. There is no doubt that parents love their children even more than the children love them. Powerful parental love is seemingly the beginning of the evolution of love; and the coming chapters will elaborate upon this cradle of all loves.

3

THE APPEARANCE OF LOVE

As the previous chapter posits, love is an evolutionary product; that is, the talent to love, the wish to love, the ability to love, and the need to be loved are somehow genetically passed on from generation to generation. But evolution has been going on for about 4 billion years. When did love appear? Was the first living creature, probably some kind of virus or microbe, capable of love? Was it equipped with the genes for love? And what about the creatures that followed it, even long after? Do fish love? After all, when we wish to describe someone as incapable of love, we say he is a "cold fish." After the fish, earth was populated by amphibians and then by reptiles. Does a lizard love? That would be hard to believe. What the microbe, fish, and lizard have in common is that they are cold-blooded and cold-feeling. Love requires warm blood. Warm blood causes warm feelings, and warm blood is a very new "invention" of evolution, being only about 150 million years old. It was brought into the world by the mammals, the last family to appear on earth and to which we belong.

What happened? All life forms that existed before the mammals—that is, all life forms on earth from 4 billion to 150 million years back—constantly needed an external source of warmth in order to function and were dependent on the sun. They could not produce their own body heat. Imagine a lizard's morning. The alarm clock goes off, it doesn't jump up, have coffee, brush its teeth, and rush to work. No. It crawls slowly out of its hole and with effort goes to bask in the sun. It is unable to start its day before that, because it does not have the energy—it cannot activate its muscles and rush to work. This is, of course, a restrictive dependence, because until it finds an external source to supply it with the ability to live, it cannot live. The lizard is like a car without fuel.

The mammal invention freed living creatures from immediate dependence on the sun. Mammals maintain their body temperature at an almost constant level throughout the day. Humans, for instance, refuel body temperature around 37 degrees centigrade throughout the day—summer or winter, morning, noon, or night, at the north pole or at the equator. This is how we achieved independence. We are no longer addicted to the sun in order to start the day. When we think of the world as the mammals found it 150 million years ago, ruled by big reptiles, giant lizards, and dinosaurs, this is a great advantage. Their rule was absolute, powerful, total—the newly arrived, tiny mammal did not have a chance on earth to find its livelihood. A small creature, such as a mouse or a shrew, could not compete against these giants for living space unless it were to outsmart them and steal out in uncharted territory—the night. Then, it could even steal one of their eggs because they were helpless, fuel-less at night, and the winnings went to those who could maintain their body heat at night. This available "niche" of nighttime is what encouraged the appearance of warm blood. And so we get an entirely new creature: one that is economically independent.

To this day, 90% of all mammals are night creatures. The night, as we have said, gave birth to warm blood. But what is the connection between warm blood and warm feelings? We were looking for warm feelings, feelings of love.

Economic independence is a privilege of the rich. When can one be independent? When one has sufficient internal sources and is not in need of external ones. Maintaining constant body temperature over 24 hours and all year long is very expensive. It requires at least two important things: (1) a lot of raw material—a lot of nutritious food; and (2) heat-creating mechanisms that transform food into the sort of energy required by our bodies' activities. This means that the new kind of creature, which has the right to economic independence, pays a steep price for it—in both materials and maintenance mechanisms. This price cannot be paid by the little ones, the newborns. These sophisticated mechanisms are not yet sufficiently ripe and active in infants. Therefore, evolution now selected the characteristic that was the most important, dramatic, and stunning of all the mammal characteristics—intensive parenting. The parents care for their young ones, who have just emerged into the world unable to look after themselves. In saying parents, we mean first and foremost mothers, who come to the aid of the little ones when they cannot cope on their own.

The supreme measure of the new motherhood is physical proximity. The mother hugs the newborn close to her body, thus performing the two functions essential to preserving its life: protection and nutrition (see Figure 2). In cuddling the newborn, she shields it from the dangers that threaten it, notably the cold and predators. At the same time, she nourishes it.

Where did this hugging come from? How did the transition from egg-laying reptiles to suckling mothers occur? We can suppose that it started when mothers kept the eggs inside their bodies for longer periods of time, before they laid them, as a sort of ongoing incubation, with the fetus developing in improved, warmer, more protected internal conditions rather than in harsh external conditions. Later, when the offspring was born, it still needed help and warmth. Lacking the ability to maintain its own body heat, it clung to mother's belly. It is possible that while on mother's belly, it attached itself to sweat or fat glands that it found there and started sucking on them, again, for support. There has been a process of functional conversion of two, four, six, and up to twelve sweat glands in mothers of the mammal family. This conversion has made them into glands that produce a slightly different liquid, not sweat, but enriched sweat, high-energy fluid, which we call milk. The baby, which emerges helpless, and still needs warmth, physical closeness, nutrition,

Figure 2
New Mammalian Motherhood: Nursing and Protecting

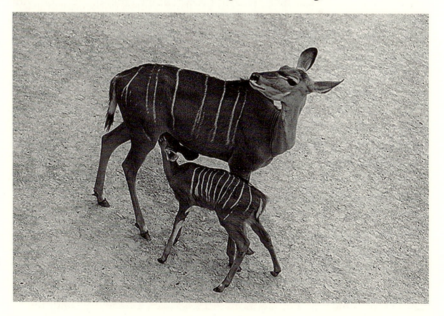

and protection, attaches itself to the sweat glands, which have become milk glands, and is nourished by high-energy fuel, sweet sweat.

These devices of suckling mothers appear today in two major variations. The first is the marsupial. We know the kangaroo, but there are some 120 types of marsupials. The newborn emerges from the belly at an early stage, under-developed and formless. It climbs up the mother's belly and drops into the pouch, where the nipples await it, full of high-energy milk, and where it spends many long months in hothouse conditions. Then it starts to peek out a bit and retreat back in, and again it peeks and retreats. It will leave the mother's pouch only when it is prepared to be an earth-bound mammal, maintaining a steady body temperature.

The second variation is the placentalia, to which we belong and which, no doubt, is the last word in this area. The placenta is a disc of blood vessels that is attached to the mother on one side and that the fetus is attached to on the other side. Thus, there is between them a perfect connection of blood vessels, which are the nutritional and growth system of the fetus. After it emerges from the womb and this disc is torn at the umbilical cord, it continues to suck milk from the sweat glands, which become high-energy glands.

Compared to the types of motherhood that were prevalent before the emergence of mammals, we have here a totally new kind: devoted, close, incessant, and intensive; this motherhood is very expensive in terms of time, energy, and risk. Why would mothers want to do it? Let's consider the mother lizard. She chooses some nice, sunny little hole in the ground, digs a bit with her tail, lays a few eggs, and goes on home. She is done. Now she is free to attend classes, go to the movies, or sun herself on the beach. If we were to approach her, and say: "No, no, ma'am. You haven't finished, you've just begun. Now you have to nurse, get up at night, change diapers, and you have to start rushing, taking care and feeding, and take him to kindergarten, drive him to school and to activities, buy him a bicycle, and send him off backpacking around the world." To which she will reply: "Oh, no! I'm not crazy." There is no motivation mechanism that will cause a female lizard to devote herself to her children. Some lizards, like the giant Komodo, not only do not care for their young, but are prepared simply to devour them, if the offspring are not quick enough to escape to the trees and hide. Ancient creatures will not take care of their children unless evolution comes along and adds something, and that something is an amazing thing—warm feeling.

Evolution selected emotionality together with intensive motherhood. The placenta and milk are expensive investments that mothers make for the sake of their kids, but they are worth nothing unless they are part of a caring, devoted, alert mother. The emotions were, and are, a necessary condition to evoke the new mother's behavior. The mammal family introduced emotionality into the world. Mammal mothers do care. Nursing mothers do not sacrifice themselves for their children. On the contrary, the children are their raison d'etre. To watch the child eat is a joy; to watch it sleep is to dissolve in pleasure. To think of any threat to the little one's well-being gives rise to deep fear; to know that the threat is over brings forth deep relief. This is the new emotional world of concerned, caring, loving mothers. In the same way that evolution selected milk glands, the womb, the birth canal, and so forth, it selected the urge, the concern, the joy and the satisfaction that motivate mothers.

In order to illustrate my claim that the first and foremost component, the very basis, of new motherhood, is physical proximity, let us consider it in some detail. In the entire mammal family, after having given birth, mothers immediately commence to lick their little ones, and they lick for a long time. The mothers then crouch over the infants most of the time, still licking them frequently and carrying them around in their teeth, on their back, or on their belly. If one of them dares to wander from the nest, they bring it back at once. This close physical contact of the infants' and the mother's dyad for 24 hours a day can go on for weeks in small mammals, for months in large mammals, and for years in monkeys. The chimpanzees, our closest relatives, continue the intimate physical contact with their young for six years and more.

What is the importance of this touch? We could learn about that if we were to separate a mother from her infants. This is prohibited in humans, of course, but we allow ourselves such experiments with rats. In an important series of research studies, conducted by the American scientist Saul Schanberg and colleagues, the mother was removed from the infants, and various physiological parameters were measured in their blood. The chain of resulting reactions was very dramatic. Half an hour of the mother's absence was enough to create significant processes. First, a high increase in the level of endorphins was recorded. Endorphin is a morphine-like substance produced in the brain, which, similar to the morphine we use, serves to calm and soothe pain and fear. But when its level increases, then as a result of mediation by an important enzyme, ornthine decarboxylase (ODC), the levels of the growth hormone and of insulin both decrease. In addition, the number of antibodies in the blood are dramatically reduced, and many more out-of-balance events take place.

What is the logic behind this chain of events? The answer is simple: emergency preparations. The orphaned little one, whose mother disappeared, feels as if abandoned in the middle of a desert, all alone and hopeless. The first thing it does is very logical. It calms itself with endorphins in order to prevent panic because panic could be its downfall. Its next action is no less logical: It starts to save its resources. If, for instance, our airplane were to crash-land in the middle of the desert, we would first count all our biscuits and ration them for as many days as possible. Similarly, we find a severe decrease of the growth hormone in the young orphans, which means that the body stops growing, and a decrease in insulin, which means that a delay of metabolism has begun. The slowing down of growth and metabolism is just like emergency rationing. We also find a reduction of antibodies in the immune system for the same reason—to save resources. The result of all these changes is arrested development. A baby, deprived of its mother and her physical touch, stops growing and is prone to disease.

Once this lesson was learned in rats, it was also tried out on human babies. In the standard premature-baby nursery, the baby is kept in sterile incubation, while the mother is released home and can come or not come to visit her baby. No touch, no mothering takes place. The investigators performed the following experiment: the premature babies were divided into two groups. One group continued with the standard program—no Mom, no touch; the other group got a new and revolutionary program: members of the team spent 15-minute periods, three times a day, stroking the babies, despite sterility rules, from the head, to the back, to the backs of their legs, over and over again. Within a few weeks of this novel style of handling prematureness, the stroked babies gained 50% more in weight than the standard babies. After all, the main job of premature babies is to gain weight. They were more alert, active, and mature, and were released from hospital at least a week earlier than the other group. Months later, they were still doing better than the infants who hadn't been touched. This experiment shows that physical proximity is the correct condition, under which development will be optimal. The magic touch signals "full steam ahead" to all major systems. In contrast, separation freezes development. Touch is also magic for the feeling mother, who obtains satisfaction and joy from it. Both the mother and baby guard this closeness with passion, nonstop. If we try to prevent it, they strongly resist. The baby screams, and the mother fights valiantly to renew physical proximity with her baby.

Evolution has planted the need for physical proximity as cerebral, neural, physiological, and psychological mechanisms, which are so strong that we can detect their power in people of all ages. We all long for touch; we feel good when it is there, and we feel bad when it is missing. In one of the first research studies in this area, the residents of an old-age home were given pets to be stroked. This was pure physical touch; there were no words to listen to. The residents who had the pets lived longer, and also improved their feelings and their health. Monkeys, like our ancient ancestors, spend hours grooming each other. Nit picking is just one function of this touch. Social communication, gossip, affirmation of family kinship, balancing of the physiological, hormonal, and rhythmic systems, blood pressure, metabolism, immune system, and more are all additional functions of touch. Touching is part and parcel of the mammals' life. Monkeys, just like people recovering from heart attacks, achieve much better results on various indicators of health when they are in pleasant company and are not lonely. The mammalian mothers were the first in evolution to feel concern about others, and they set the cradle for the evolution of love, the dependence of every individual on proximity, belonging, being cuddled. Throughout evolution, love, first as touch and then as a rich cluster of loving behaviors, has become a need, and even a prerequisite, for physiological and psychological well-being. This is true mainly in babies, but extends to humans of all ages. This love was born in the mammalian relationship between mother and infant.

4

MATERNAL LOVE IN HUMANS

Love was introduced into the behavioral repertoire of creatures on earth by mothers of the mammal family, who were sensitive to their helpless infants. Motherhood is the self-mobilizing to help a young offspring. The new talent for warm and loving feeling that accompanies motherhood is cast into passion and satisfaction. Maternal concern, maternal motivation, maternal experience—all reach their peak in humans because of particularly harsh conditions, under which more intensive, more devoted, and more loving motherhood was required. The human species would not have been able to evolve without such enthusiastic and determined motherhood. What were these harsh conditions?

The first push was climatic change. About 8 million years ago, as a result of tectonic activity, Africa was torn apart by the "Rift Valley," which separated our ape forefathers into two groups. On the west side, the same old friendly, humid, warm climate continued, and that is where our brothers, the chimpanzees, live to this day. On the east, conditions gradually altered, and the region turned arid and dry with cool nights. The rising of the rift banks along with the Himalayan Mountains that rose at about the same time in Central Asia, boxed in a new air circulation system. Its winds slowly dried out the ancient paradise. Vegetation, which thrived in the previous climate, was now subject to the same withering that occurs when we purchase a plant in a hothouse and bring it home with us. It exchanges humidity and warmth for the coolness and dryness of our home and does not fare well. That is what happened to the tropical forest, which had covered great parts of East Africa in that ancient time. The forest retreated and shrank.

For the apes who inhabited the eastern forest, the bough they were sitting on was sawed off. On the western side, where the forest stood firm, apes continued their previous life and look today much as they looked then. The chimpanzee, for instance, has not changed much for millions of years. Humans, on the other hand, who shared the same parents with the chimpanzee 8 million years ago, changed immensely. This change began when our ancient forefathers were forced to give up the benign forest and adapt to life on the mosaic land of sparse woods and savanna, which replaced it. Savanna is an arid, open area covered by high grass, scarred with few, barren trees. The first question the ape on the savanna must ask itself is: What do I have for breakfast? And after it copes with extremely severe mutations needed for living on an entirely different food-basket, it must cope with additional questions involving where to sleep, where to leave the children, where to hide when a predator shows up. It is impossible to quickly climb to a tree top and evade the tiger, especially when there is neither tree nor tree top. The mental conception of environment, which the brain builds, interprets, and makes decisions about, must be modified, so that it is adapted to survival in an open area rather than a forest. Senses and behavioral techniques must change. The new environment suddenly presented the ape with almost unappeasable demands. And when life becomes difficult, it is close to impossible for the little ones—the infants—unless their mothers come to their salvation.

The physiological mechanisms of the young are as yet underdeveloped; they cannot maintain their body heat, their metabolism is still shaky, and their immune system is weak. They can face this tough transition only if they have a loving, caring, devoted mother. We are all in outstanding debt to a long chain of passionate, compassionate, merciful, generous mothers, generation after generation, who took humankind from the forest haven to this day.

When humankind started the journey the anthropologist Yves Coppens calls it the "East Side Story," which differentiated it from the rest of the apes, two major distinguishable characteristics appeared and evolved. The first, in timetable terms as well as in significance for future human evolution, is rising to bipedality. Humans are the only mammals that walk on two feet. Some biologists call this very special, very strange walk a "ridiculous walk." The second characteristic is the large head, which contains a brain three times bigger than the ancestor's brain. Chimpanzees, whom we resembled until not so long ago, have a 450-cubic centimeter brain, whereas our brains grew within the last 3 million years to the size of 1350 cubic centimeters on the average. Tripling the brain's size and standing upright are most important features of the human species, and both are closely related to motherhood. For millions of years humans lived as gatherer-hunters. Women gathered roots, cereals, bulbs, and berries, while men hunted game. Scavenging was perhaps the first step, and raw meat followed. A fierce debate was spread over decades about the correct ratio of booty parts. Did women contribute more to the family table, or were men the providers? The answer was, of course, a matter of political correctness or incorrectness. Escaping the mines of political correctness, it is simply suggested that both women and men, in the harsh, empty savanna, had to carry their gathering-hunting booty a long distance home to share and to feed the kids. And that is what really matters, since the ape who filled its hands with booty stood up, rose to bipedality, and walked on two feet in order to free its hands. Apparently, the first human characteristic appeared as a parental behavior. Motherhood backed up bipedality. The same goes for the large brain.

A big brain is certainly a big merit. The mental abilities of humans—their wisdom, their minds, their cunning, planning, and scheming—have made them into apes, who might survive in the savanna. But there is a fly in the ointment. This huge wisdom requires a huge head, and that is a new problem for mother. Mother was accustomed to deliver through the birth canal a head that would grow to the size of 450 cubic centimeters, and now we come and ask her to deliver a head three times as big, a head that will grow to the size of 1350 cubic centimeters. Mother cannot do it; she would be ripped apart. These clever babies tore their mothers apart during birth. This is worse than "I will greatly multiply thy pain . . . in pain thou shalt bring forth children." As promised in the Book of Genesis it was literally impossible to give birth. A solution had to be found in order to maintain the tremendous advantage of a clever son, since as the Book of Proverbs states, a "wise son makes a glad father, but a foolish son is his mother's grief." A solution which will keep the mother alive, because a wise son who is an orphan can bring no joy to his father, and also stands no chance to survive the harsh conditions of the savanna.

Evolution selected a solution to this problem in two parallel moves. The first was enlarging the female's hip width. On its way out of the womb, the baby passes through an opening in the woman's pelvis. This is the critical moment. A big head, which cannot pass through, will rip the mother apart and kill her. But if the opening is large enough, then a big head can emerge through it. And so, in a dramatic and acute process, natural selection enlarged the woman's pelvis opening more and more, until it suited the wise infant. To this day, woman's hip width distinguishes her from man. Early in infancy, even as a fetus, a baby girl's pelvis is wider than a boy's. In adults we can see this distinction externally. A woman's hips, and especially her waist-to-hip ratio, are part of her secondary sexual traits, and it is interesting to note that they have become arousing, attractive traits. A man is attracted to a woman's wide pelvis and to her feminine walk, which derives from this very hip width. A woman's walk was transformed first because of uprightness and then, second, to enable a wider passage for birth. Both changes caused woman's hips to swing while walking, and this has become an attractive sexual sign. Man is attracted to this sign as if it says: a woman with this kind of walk can be a mother; therefore, it is worthwhile to have sex with her and produce offspring. The capacity for successful motherhood has become a symbol of sexuality. Femininity is head over heels maternity.

The second parallel step that evolution took to solve the problem of the big head was to slow down the development rate of the fetus in the womb. Richard Leakey, descendant of the famous Kenyan anthropologist family, suggests that pregnancy used to last twelve months and that it was shortened to nine months because an increasingly bigger head had to be delivered through the birth canal. Most scientists claim, however, that pregnancy in the human past took nine months, quite similar to the chimpanzee timetable, but now the fetus develops more slowly. So that at the end of nine months, we get a smaller head. This solution raised a new problem: the fetus is less mature and more helpless when it is born. The human infant is apparently the most helpless neonate in all of nature, and there is none other like it in its total and continuous need of its mother.

When we compare the level of maturity of chimpanzee and human neonates, the gap between them is as much as two years on a number of indicators. The human newborn lags behind the chimpanzee neonate by pace of development inside the womb, so a lot has to be done on the outside. The helpless human infant faces a long road of growing and maturing, a road no one can travel alone. Who will guide and support the helpless infant if not its mother, an endlessly loving and devoted mother, who is willing to do anything anytime. In the arid, cold, hostile, predator-infested savanna of the gushing rivers, the freezing nights, and the pitfalls, without clinics or doctors, social workers, Pampers or milk substitutes, no infant could last if it did not have a loving, attentive, responding, devoted mother.

Demography also tells the tale of maternal love. For millions of years the increase in the human population rate stood at zero, and it is only during the last few thousand years that a huge expansion began, to the point of population explosion today. Before this boom of civilization, the count of the entire human species was in the tens of thousands, maybe hundreds of thousands, and it did not increase. Let us consider this matter from one mother's point of view.

The mother probably breastfed every baby for about four years. Lactation prevents an additional pregnancy by means of the hormone prolactin, which suppresses ovulation. Mammalian motherhood is so expensive that natural selection added contraceptives to its evolution. (It's true, we all know someone who became pregnant while breast-feeding. The behavior of breast-feeding mothers of the !Kung-Sun African tribe might indicate the reason for this hitch: A !Kung woman carries her infant close to her body 24 hours a day, and it sates its hunger in "gulps" about every 10 to 15 minutes. As long as the infant stimulates the nipples a neural signal tells the brain to produce more prolactin. Modern mothers, graduates of Dr. Spock, are convinced that there must be a timetable for "meals" of every four or five hours. These hours are time enough to significantly reduce the prolactin level and to enable pregnancy, despite breast-feeding.) Birth intervals were thus about four years long. Assuming a woman had become fertile at the age of 15 and could give birth until she was 40, an average woman therefore had six children in her lifetime. But if the population increase rate remains zero, then of six children born, only two survive. Mother is destined to lose two-thirds of her children.

Infant and child mortality has always been part of human life. Actually, death accompanied childhood until the twentieth century. In Europe of the Middle Ages, 30% of all children died before the age of five, and so it went on to the nineteenth century. In a marvelous biography of Tolstoy, Henri Troyat describes how Lev and Sonya Tolstoy dealt with the death of five out of their twelve children. The time was the second half of the nineteenth century, and this family was well-to-do. So although we are far from the savanna, death is still present. As child after child dies, their hearts break with their sorrow, in particular mother Sonya's heart. This woman shows remarkable fortitude and courage, as she rises again after yet another child's demise. Only at the end, when her little Vanya, her fifth to die, breathes his last does she lose her vigor. With his death something in her soul is extinguished.

Were the mothers of the savanna or of the Middle Ages, or Sonya Tolstoy, who could face the deaths of so many children less vulnerable than we are? On the contrary, their enormous caring, their deep sensitivity to the child's life and death, managed to keep one or two of the children alive against all odds. When an average of two-thirds of the children are doomed to die, only an extremely attentive and responsive mother can succeed in keeping one-third alive. By means of genetic heredity, these mothers passed on their caring and sensitivity to be expressed in us.

Motherhood, mainly human, but also the entire mammalian motherhood, has become such a strong force in evolution that every female is equipped with a multitude of traits, behaviors, and inclinations that constitute motherhood. This is akin to comprehensive insurance. It is very difficult to find a mother who fails in all aspects of motherhood. If she doesn't do very well in getting the child to eat enough, then she is diligent in taking it to the doctor; if she doesn't see to it that the child gets good grades at school, then she skillfully pushes it to play the violin. Evolution was so zealous about motherhood that many women are blessed with "excesses" which they discharge in charity work, help to the needy, the sick, feeding animals, or caring for someone.

Another example of the depth of evolutionary investment in mothers can be found in a reciprocal behavior which we can call the stimulant–response system. When the baby sends stimulating signals, the mother returns appropriate responses. For instance, a baby does not learn how to cry; it just cries since the ability to cry is built in before birth. A mother does not have to learn how to respond to an infant's crying; she just jumps up whenever she hears her baby. She wakes up out of a deep sleep the moment she hears those alerting sounds. Furthermore, her breasts fill up with milk in reaction. The stimulant is received in the ear and rises to the brain, whereupon the brain sends a signal to the breast by means of the hormone prolactin. Within the two or three minutes it takes for her to reach the baby, her breasts are full of milk.

Another example is the smile. No one teaches a baby to smile, but when it does oblige, the grownup feels like a million dollars. And what won't grownups do to win a baby's smile? They crowd around it, they make faces, chirp, twitter, and squeak—and they are filled with joy when the smile arrives. Yet another example is clinging and touch. When the baby clings to the parent's body, the parent is filled to overflowing with warmth, tenderness, and happiness, and therefore becomes eager to nurture. This is the actual meaning of the stimulant–response system. The baby is equipped with behaviors that motivate the parent to continue to give care. Indeed, these behaviors motivate the parents, because they themselves are equipped with the ability to receive these signals and respond to them "correctly," in a way that will raise the offspring's chances of success. Evolution was so hard at work on this issue—so serious, so deep, and especially so with human mothers—because motherhood was the condition for the survival of humans under all the hardships that had befallen them on the way from forest to savanna.

5

MOTHERHOOD SPEAKS

The evolutionary story of humans, a part of which is reviewed in the previous chapter, is somewhat like the tale of banishment from paradise in the Book of Genesis. The exit from the lavish tropical forest to the arid savanna suggests the expulsion from the Garden of Eden to the hostile world. In Genesis the sin was knowledge, and the punishment was exile. In our story, knowledge is no sin, but a big prize, although it has a price. The human brain grew to three times the size of the ape's brain, and wisdom does involve pain—"in pain thou shalt bring forth children." The mother gives birth in agony due to the bigger head, which knows so much. Some might argue that it would have been better to forgo painful wisdom, to remain in a fool's paradise, but it is a fact that today's human has the biggest brain (relative to body size) of any other living creature. The big head embodies human preeminence.

If we were to choose the one basic, important component of human preeminence, which might be the source of all humankind's unique abilities, it would be speech. Indeed, humans have preeminence in language. All human accomplishments would not have been possible if not for speech. Our culture, consciousness, awareness, technology, art, and sociability are all based on language. Speech is communication, and that is something our predecessors in the evolutionary chain also had. As a matter of fact, even the simplest creatures communicate, but at the beginning it was silent communication, through scent or visual signs that can be smelled or seen but not heard. When the mammals, creatures of the night, introduced the important innovation of warm blood and in its footsteps—devoted maternal care of the offspring—they needed communication by sound, audio communication.

As was stated in Chapter 2, warm blood gave mammals the opportunity to take hold of the available night-niche from which they prospered. When we come to make the connection between the vital need for close contact between mother and child and the darkness of night, it is apparent that communication between mother and child cannot rely solely on sight. The language of sound was, therefore, selected in mammals, the devoted parents. In this way, telecommunication came to the aid of close connections.

Mothers and pups communicate by sounds, whereas mothers and children communicate by speech. Since this close contact has become a condition of life and death, an infant without extremely tight communication with its mother cannot survive. To this day, even in the remarkably comfortable conditions we have for raising children, the feeling of need of physical proximity between mother and child, and the fear and pain related to separation, are one of the most powerful feelings we know. Auditory communication evolved with them in the mammalian family. The infant calls its mother; the mother calls her infant.

These calls of separation and unity are the basis of auditory communication. Cries of separation are a quintessential characteristic of all mammal infants when they are abandoned. In my home, I raised two dogs, mother and daughter. For an unusually long time, the mother was extraordinarily compassionate, delicate, and maternal, looking after her offspring for ten whole years. Then one day she was run over. In the afternoon and evening of that day, the orphan, by now ten years old, searched for her. Lacking communication I couldn't explain to her. At five the next morning I was awakened by heartbreaking cries of separation, "ooh, ooh," or in our language, "Mummy, come to me." The orphan cried like that every morning at 5:00 for a month. Perhaps these were 30 days of a desperate effort to reunite, or perhaps they were 30 mornings of mourning. And then she stopped.

When we review the history of communication, we distinguish between two types of sounds in monkeys. The first type is the cry or whimper of the infant when it is abandoned, something like "aaah," which also serves many adults as a separation call. The second type of sound is clucking. When, for instance, the infants' lips disconnect from the nipple, there is a "tsk" sound, or when the mother wants to catch her infant's attention, to encourage it to go on suckling, she makes the same sound. These are sounds we can also hear in humans between mother and child, and they are the ancient roots of the two basic units of any human language to this day: open vowels ("aaah") and consonants ("tsk"). Vowels and consonants are the basis of language, but in apes, that's all there is. Human neonates, on the other hand, start out with raw vowels and consonants, but a few months later they begin to murmur. Syllables, as yet meaningless, emerge. The fact that all human babies murmur and that even deaf babies murmur shows that, as a result of the special evolution of humans in the area of communication, human language is implanted as a premature infrastructure in every child's brain. At birth, the neonate is equipped with genetic instructions, which construct neural-cerebral centers and pathways, that enable it to be exposed to language. Deaf babies stop to murmur after a number of months. A hearing child, when not exposed to talk, will also stop murmuring. However, if it is surrounded by spoken language, then by virtue of the unique evolution of the human species, it is able to absorb words and to cast its initial murmurs into meaningful verbal forms.

Human evolution worked on language or on communication in a special way and transformed speaking into more precise, sophisticated, and superb communication. This, perhaps, points to the mother's supreme obligation under the severe savanna conditions to better understand their infants and to answer their needs precisely. This is what language makes possible—to figure out whether a baby is crying because it is too cold or too hot, because it is hungry or thirsty, because it is afraid or in pain. To this day we hear mothers sigh over their infants and say: "I wish he could talk," because then they would be able to understand him better.

The American writer Sydney Mellen, in his book *The Evolution of Love* (which gave me not only the title of my book, but also a great deal of inspiration), supports the idea that mothers stimulated the development of human language, with research findings about the advantages of women in verbal skills. Again and again many dozens of studies from all over the world, found that females, as a global group, have a clear advantage over males, as a global group, in various verbal parameters. If we take women and men of all ages, and measure a number of language parameters, such as at what age babies begin to talk, their verbal fluency, their vocabulary richness, their mastery of grammar, spelling, and pronunciation, then women as a group excel men as a group in almost any criterion. Speech was selected as yet another tool of attentive motherhood.

The evolution of language, the best of human preeminence, is related to yet another unique human phenomenon. Our right side is stronger and dominant over our left; there is no such clear, consistent preference of sides in other creatures. Humans mostly favor the right hand over the left, and the right foot and right eye. Both phenomena—speech and dominance—are related to each other and to mothers. How? Mothers tend to hold their infants on their left side, though surely not one mother is aware of it. If we were to line up a hundred mothers and hand a baby to one after the other, we would find that 70 to 80% would take the baby and hold it to their left side, embraced to their hearts (see Figure 3). If we were to perform the same experiment on one hundred men, we would get completely different results. Some of them would absolutely refuse to take the baby, others would swing it over their heads, and the rest would distribute equally between left and right.

Taking baby to the left seems to be a genetically implanted phenomenon. It is not due to right-hand dominance; on the contrary, taking infants to the left side came first in evolution. Laterality came later. Left-handed women also hold their infant on their left, as do apes who have no significant preference of arms. A number of proposals have been made to explain this leftist bias, which we will not go into here. Let us settle for the one notion that many researchers have accepted and that does not detract from the importance of all other explanations. Apparently, cuddling the infant to the left side was selected because it allows the infant's ear to be next to the mother's heartbeat, to make it feel better, and to give it the feeling of returning home. For nine months its home was the womb, where the heartbeat was heard loud and clear. It returns home to the familiar, everlasting pace, and so it calms down. The rhythm of the heart comforts the infant. Mothers unconsciously make use of this very

Figure 3
Eastern and Western Mothers Take Infants to Their Left

rhythm in many ways to soothe an infant. They rock it in a cradle or a carriage, they sway back and forth while hugging it, they gently pat its back or behind.

Music can also soothe, especially music that has a rhythm similar to the heartbeat—about 70 beats per minute. Actually, the average tempo of all human music, from rough rap to mourning pavane, is 70. A calm infant is healthier and better developed. Moreover, a calm infant does not scream, and that gives it and its mother a better chance of survival on the danger-ridden savanna, swarming with predators, That is how this maternal inclination was selected. By holding the infant in the left arm, the right arm was freed to improve in areas that females have traditionally specialized in: gleaning berries, roots, and bulbs, then doing delicate handiwork, and at much later periods perhaps engaging in agriculture. To this day women have an advantage over men in tasks that require delicate manual dexterity. Generally, women are better at handicrafts, and their handwriting is superior to men's.

If the right hand is active, it sustains that part of the brain that dominates and gives it instructions. As the brain dominates the body in cross-check neural pathways, its left hemisphere activates the right hand and responds to its activity. This process can be observed in two ways; first as an evolutionary process in which the right hand, free and active, and the left motor cortex of the brain grow and consolidate more in women; and second as a developmental process as observed in the lifetime of a single human. If we exercise, say, three fingers meticulously every day, within a few weeks we will find, under the microscope, growth of the brain area that activates these three fingers. In this way exercise improves our abilities. This developmental process recapitulates the evolutionary process, which occurred slowly over millions of years.

The more a woman uses her free hand, the more she becomes right-handed. Speech, a sophisticated human communication, is a delicate praxis of the mouth. The mouth is unique to the body in that unlike an arm or a leg, it is not on the side of the body, but on a central line, nor is it one of a pair. In activating central organs of the body, it is difficult to use both hemispheres, both halves of the brain, in such perfect harmony so that a function as sophisticated as human speech can emerge. Production of speech involves the amazing number of 140,000 muscular-neural events per second. Therefore, in order to produce a delicate praxis of speech, of the tongue, the lips, inhaling and exhaling, one hemisphere was selected to act precisely and uniformly. Perhaps because of women's liberated right hand, evolution selected the left hemisphere, where delicate praxis is already highly perfected. Thus, the left hemisphere in the human brain has become the speaking hemisphere. Both human speech centers, Broca's area, which produces speech, and Wernicke's area, which deciphers the meaning of speech, are located in the left hemisphere.

The areas of the brain that produce speech are geographically close to the right-hand delicate praxis area, especially in women. Men's speech regions are more scattered.

In describing the development of speech by means of female evolution, I do not claim that men did not evolve in the same way. Indeed, children of both sexes inherit all of their mother's selected genes. Speech genes are passed on from parents to all their children. What I claim is that natural selection, which just "loved" the appearance of speech, accelerated it first in women, apparently by means of feminine tools, the powerful growth factors and estrogens. That is why they still possess some related advantages.

In its evolution, language has become our most prominent mental activity. Words are our world, and indeed, since the moment we learn to speak, we never stop. We speak endlessly, to the point that speech seems to be the sum of our mental activity. Actually, however, the main mental activity of children and of earlier evolutionary creatures is visual. They see pictures and process images. Only after having acquired language, words, which are so very powerful, become the child's central mental activity. Following the development of speech, the left, speaking, hemisphere becomes the dominant hemisphere in the brain. As it matures, it becomes stronger than the right hemisphere. A child is born with no dominance of either side. Only after having attained language skills and using them more and more, and only after they have become a central tool of the child's cerebral processes, only then, between the ages of four and six, does the right hand become stronger than the left, and most children become right-handed. Speech creates right dominance. Looking for the dependence of handedness on speech, I conducted a study in 1994 on four-year-olds and found a high and significant correlation (r = .88; $p.$ < 01) between children's vocabulary and their right-handedness. The better talker was also more right-handed, and girls were better than boys in both vocabulary and right-handedness. When a child starts speaking earlier, the left hemisphere grows to dominate the right one faster and eventually establishes stronger right-hand preference. At the age of four children display this process in "real time."

The idea that right-handedness is just a byproduct of language is so appealing that all we have said before about women's free right hand may be superfluous. The decisive evidence could be the research on handedness in children adopted by animals. Without human language, those children probably would have no hand preference either. Unfortunately, I never obtained any information to test the hypothesis. Some support of the idea comes from study of healthy deaf students whose rate of left-handedness increases to 28% compared to 10% in population. But after all, they do use some sort of language, and the speech areas in their brains are active. Returning to motherhood, we find that women have some interesting advantages over men in spoken, written, and read language, as well as in right-handedness, and the logical mind starts thinking about estrogens. If language was promoted by mothers and right dominance was promoted by speaking mothers, then estrogen is present. Some 10% of all people today are not right-handed. Some of them strongly prefer the left side, while others exhibit mixed dominance. In a survey I conducted among 1,681 adults in Israel in 1994, I found that women are more right-handed than men. About 12% of all men are left-handed compared to only 8% of all women. Within the right-handed group, right-handedness is more pronounced, more powerful, and more ingrained in women than in men.

When the left hemisphere is not strong enough, difficulties in speech and language skills are evident. Stuttering and dyslexia are two very well-known examples of such difficulties. Both of these disorders occur mainly in boys; in fact, 90% of all victims are boys. The peak of these language disorders occurs at an age when the left hemisphere is supposed to take over and produce the dominance of the right hand. It is at this age, between four and six, that dyslexia and stuttering appear. If we take the left-handers as a group and measure their rate of dyslexia, we will find it to be ten times higher than in right-handers; that is, people whose left hemisphere is weaker than average are less talkative and less right-handed.

At times, the left hemisphere is not dominant, not just because it is weak but because the right one is stronger. The right hemisphere specializes in spatial perception, which is a wonderful gift of artists, architects, mathematicians, musicians, and chess-players. A long list of famous artists—Michelangelo and Leonardo Da Vinci, Rubens, Titian, Van Gogh, Mondrian, Rembrandt, and Rodin—were all left-handed. Moreover, Da Vinci was known for his mirror-writing, and in our day he would have been called dyslexic.

The basic evolutionary reasons for spatial perception talents are navigation and orientation. Men, like many other males in nature, are more mobile than women, and as a group, surpass women in their orientation and navigation abilities. This talent is developed through the androgenic male hormones in the brain of the fetus, and as a result men have a distinct group advantage over women in spatial perception behaviors. Thus it is that men surpass women in chess, in music composition, mathematics, painting, and architecture. And among the chess-players, composers, mathematicians, and architects, we will find a stronger inclination than in the general population towards left-handedness and speech difficulties. For this reason, the Faculty of Mathematics at Oxford University, for example, had three times more lecturers who suffered dyslexia in childhood than the Faculty of Social Studies. In other words the left hemisphere of Oxford mathematicians is not very strong as opposed to the right one, and so they are good at mathematics and bad at speech. Thus, the femininity of language, as well as of right-handedness becomes even more salient by its masculine reversal.

If the dominance of the left hemisphere is related to motherhood, we can posit that whereas the spatial talents in the right hemisphere were developed through masculine hormones—androgens—the verbal talents in the left hemisphere were developed by feminine hormones—estrogens. Primitive monkeys such as the lemur, perhaps earlier than monkeys, demonstrate an interesting difference between the sexes. They have no speech and no dominance of any side, but when eating, females prefer the right hand and males the left. We could make the assumption that masculine hormones such as testosterone sustain the right, spatial hemisphere and that it is therefore stronger in males—hence their preference of the left hand. On the other side, the feminine hormones, estrogens, foster the left hemisphere, and it is stronger in females. All this occurred before the advent of speech. So when the human species began to speak, it might have been mothers who promoted it, and the estrogens reinforced the left, speaking, hemisphere to the point that the right side became predominant. Admittedly, men also speak, but a little less fluently than women, for they are less motherly.

6

MATERNAL LOVE AS A MODEL

At some point in the evolutionary line of organisms, from the first simple microbes to the rich variety of complex creatures alive today, maternal love appeared as the first love on earth. Maternal love is both the first love created by evolution and the first love that everyone experiences. This dual primacy has made maternal love the prototype of all subsequent loves we will know in the course of our life span; all subsequent loves seemingly draw the materials required from this primordial love. The hormones, neural and cerebral processes, feelings, drive, and behavior that enact mother-infant relationships are repeated in subsequent loves, just as they were in the first one.

The Floating Opera, an intriguing book by the American author John Barth, offers a fine illustration of this idea through its description of an amazing experience. As a 17-year-old recruit, following a too short basic training, Barth was sent to the trenches in Europe during the First World War. As soon as he got to the front, he found himself in the midst of infernal gunfire, an artillery barrage that left him senseless, confused, and disoriented. At one point, he lost contact with his comrades and saw no one in his vicinity. Trembling from fear, standing on all fours in the thick mud of a shell-crater, to his surprise, he then discovered another man wallowing in misery with him. The two fell on each other's necks, hugging and kissing for long minutes, refusing to disconnect. They then shared whatever each possessed in cigarettes, biscuits, and other provisions. Still holding each other, they now recognized that one was American and the other German. Although they were enemies, the two soldiers continued to cling to each other, until their fear faded. No longer terrified animals with lost bearings, they had become human again. Despite their lack of a common language, they communicated and laughed, were happy, and had a significant dialogue. When one fell asleep, the other watched, realizing that the love he felt for this filthy creature was stronger than any love he had felt for anyone or anything in his entire life. Barth identified this love as that of "a lioness watching over her cubs"; this unique experience had probably managed to tap into the real source of love. This unusual meeting created a maternal experience for these two young bachelors, not yet fathers. In spite of being enemies and in spite of their sex, physical contact in times of danger activated the very hormones, neural pathways, and brain nuclei that compose the loving maternal experience. (Both sexes possess all the genes, brain areas, and hormones; it is only the volume of their activity that varies.)

Subsequent use of the sources of initial love is performed through yet another mechanism, that of imprinting. The child must be loved during its childhood in order to be able to love in adulthood. This phenomenon was observed in the famous experiments of the primatologists Margaret and Harry Harlow with Rhesus monkeys. An infant denied maternal love cannot, in adulthood, build any sort of relationship, whether social, sexual, or parental. Usually, there are no children who are totally denied love, but some get more and some get less. And there are, of course, different types of maternal love. These styles and quality of maternal love are imprinted on the child's brain, and in adulthood the inclination is to reconstruct the same style and gestures and to use the same words. Mothers sometimes catch themselves saying to their kids what their mothers used to say to them and what they so hated. Imprinting is stronger than one's will, even stronger than one's decisions.

Falling in love is a form of regression. When we fall in love, we reconstruct our infancy. A typical example are two teenagers who for a long time haven't needed physical contact, hugs, and kisses from their parents, and in fact can hardly stand any physical touch from them. Feeling independent, they take off together to a rock concert, sleep on the beach, fall in love, and start acting like babies, cooing endearments to each other like lovey, sweetie, honey, and pet. Most of the endearments we use are actually baby clucking. These youngsters cannot think of separation; one day apart seems like death to them. Their need for physical proximity is so strong that they cannot disunite. Indeed, separation means death to the infant. People in love also tend to put their partners on a pedestal and to see them as larger than life, much as an infant relies on a parent. One of the common difficulties encountered in married life stems from the fact that at first the partner is perceived as almost godly, and then come disillusionment and disenchantment. But most marital problems are caused by the disappointment and pain that maternal love imprinted on the child's brain.

Modern mothers do their children an injustice. Ancient mothers in our evolutionary line, apes, hominids, and prehistoric homo mothers, kept their infants close to themselves for four to six years. In contrast, many modern mothers leave the baby very early in its life. They go out to work and return in the afternoon, and then the children are left again for the whole night. Our babies experience separation every day and night of their lives. The pain of detachment in babies, whose physiological and psychological outcomes are described in Chapter 3, exacts a very high price even after half an hour, not to mention longer separations. Modern cultures are raising generations of people, who are experiencing an extremely painful detachment in infancy. The pain is assimilated and imprinted, and they will then go on to become a generation of adults, whose separation anxiety is one of the most powerful influences in their lives.

Separation anxiety grows markedly in a couple's life. Each strives to cling to the other, and at the same time each fears and bewares the pain of a future separation, which does not as yet exist but already hurts because separations from mother are imprinted on the brain and are remembered. For many who find it difficult to form and maintain a relationship, separation fear is particularly powerful. Separation fear is a major factor in many psychological and psychiatric disorders.

Infants' brains are imprinted by specific mothers, with their own style or individuality, for better or worse. A good mother who bestows security and love, and lots of warmth, attachment, and physical proximity, will certainly make her child's future relations with herself and its future partner much easier. Conversely, a cold, hostile mother imprints on the child's brain an experience of difficult, humiliating, rejecting, painful love. That pain becomes the meaning of love imprinted in its brain. This child will grow up to be, say, a handsome young man, sought after by all the girls, and instead of any of the kind, warm-hearted beauties, he will choose the cold, hostile one. And when a friend asks him: "Tell me, how can you do it? Of all the great girls around here, why choose the witch?" He will say: "You know what? I know she's a witch, but she turns me on." When he says "turns me on" he hits exactly on the relevant neural-cerebral process, since imprinting is recorded onto neural circuits in the brain, and we must turn these circuits on by electric current, while awakening love until it pleases. In order to turn them on, the experience today has to be similar, in at least one feature to the imprinted experience, and the witch reminds him, in at least one feature, of mother. Maybe just by being a redhead, but she must remind him of his mother.

Here again is a common difficulty in marital relations. Children who have a bad mother imprinted on their brains are children to whom love should be related to pain and anger. Pain and anger subsequently surface in the couple's life, with no realistic basis whatsoever, by means of the mechanism that psychologists call projection. The adult finds in marriage all the hurt and pain familiar from childhood because that is what love means; that is the model from which to draw the feelings, the definition, and the reactions toward the present relationship. The pattern of the neural circuits imprinted on the brain under the heading "love" includes rejection, insult, and humiliation. When his "on-turning" mate asks him to take out the trash, he loses his cool: "Why is it always me with the trash? Is that all I mean to you? Is that all you want me for?" This is a difficult path for a relationship, and a chain of projections of this kind can cause divorce. After the divorce, when seeking a candidate for chapter two, he will try to find someone who turns him on, and if he does, then she is liable again to turn on the pain and anger imprinted by his mother, and he is destined to transfer these onto wife number two, three, and four. (Using a man, as opposed to a woman, is incidental. Both sexes experience maternal love as initial imprinting, and both will revive it over and over again in later loves.)

Different mothers imprint different flavors for love, from sweet to bitter. But the primacy of maternal love is universal in both the evolutionary and the personal developmental sense. Due to its primacy and its vigor, love has become an unquenchable thirst that stays with us till the day we die. This craving is wired in our brains as a repetitive behavior pattern. The yearning for an embracing, promising, comforting, responding, accepting, entreating love is endless. Most people experience this longing as unattainable. The desperate attempts to receive love from our mate are usually disappointing and certainly are never completely fulfilled. They are doomed to be unfulfilled for the very reason they exist. The longing is for a mother, and the mate is no mother (mates also long for motherly love). The adult seeking motherly love is no longer an infant and, therefore, cannot be satisfied. But the profound attention evolution paid to motherly love and to the longing for it made love into a Utopia for everyone's deepest craving.

The mother–child relationship is paradoxical. The mother uses the means of physical proximity. She holds the child close to protect and nourish it. But the end of these means is the opposite—to launch her offspring to independence and to encourage the reproduction of grandchildren. Two contradictory mechanisms are thus implanted in humans: clutching and dispatching—and their mirror reflections are the desire to be held close and the desire to be dispatched to independence. These mechanisms greatly balance each other. Evolutionary success is unlikely if one is stronger than the other. If the clutching mechanism is stronger, the child will forever be tied to its mother's apron strings, will not become independent and will not provide grandchildren. If the dispatching mechanism is stronger and the infant flies high too soon, it will not survive.

A flowing balance swings between the two mechanisms from the moment the baby is born until adulthood, and the proportions of dependence and clutching, as opposed to independence and dispatching, vary. As the child grows older, a greater emphasis on independence is expected. When the balance is violated in favor of clutching, the opposite mechanism kicks in and acts in order to prevent absorption and symbiosis of the child into the mother. When the balance is breached in favor of dispatching, warning bells ring in the warm, safe, protected haven of motherhood to prevent the loss of any vessel in stormy seas. The balance must change with age, and since any child and any parent is equipped with contradicting, mirroring inclinations, and since each one is a different and unique person, some degree of conflict is present throughout childhood.

Not surprisingly, the peak of the conflict is reached in adolescence. This is the moment of truth in the conflict between nestling and spreading wings. But a form of this conflict also enters into adult life in subsequent loves, as a common struggle between our separation anxiety, on the one hand, and our fear of being swallowed up, on the other. We are afraid to be assimilated by the other; we do not want to lose our individuality and identity, to lose our independence. An observing eye will notice an uneasy game among many couples, one rising and the other descending according to the mate's behavior. If our mate develops an interest in other people, places, or topics, we feel threatened and demand his or her return. The opposite is also true, so that when our mate does not leave us alone and wants to do everything together, we feel stifled and burdened, and we find ourselves performing maneuvers of evasion.

An additional psychological difficulty, related to motherhood, is depression. Women suffer from depression much more than men; some say twice as much, and others up to six times as much. Let us, for example, consider "major depression" as defined by the Diagnostic and Statistical Manual of Mental Disorders, DSM IV. To be labeled as a major depression, a number of severe criteria have to be satisfied; notably, many weeks of sadness, lack of appetite, sleeplessness, and attention disorders. Yet, statistics indicate that over 20% of women will suffer a major depression at some time in their lives, as opposed to less than 10% of men.

With regard to postpartum depression, the figures are even more impressive. No man gets after-delivery depression, whereas if we delete the severe psychotic disease erroneously called postpartum depression (it should have been called postpartum psychosis) and take into account only the slight depression experienced by many mothers after giving birth, we will reach the rate of 65 to 70%. These figures put after-birth depression within the limits of normal phenomena. How can we explain this? Depression is a normal reaction to loss, separation, or threat of separation. If one is sensitive to attachment, one is sensitive to its loss. If one knows how to make a bond and maintain it, one will ache for it and feel deeply depressed when it is severed. We cannot have a relationship with a block of wood, and a block of wood will feel no pain when we abandon it. Depression, in this sense, is like pain. It signals when something goes wrong. It calls upon us to do something, to change something and to set things right. Whoever cannot feel pain will be hurt; whoever cannot feel depression will remain alone in his appointed times. Women are equipped with the ability to feel depression more than men because of their higher sensitivity to the bond with their infant. Birth enhances this maternal ability to its summit.

One of the factors in both attachment and depression is the hormone prolactin. As noted earlier, its most well-known function is the production of milk in the breast. A less well known function is to accelerate the wish and need of physical proximity. Prolactin plays an important role in both seeking close contact and lactating, the two major principles of motherhood. Prolactin activity can also be found in nonnursing males, aimed at physical proximity to the offspring. We can inject a rat with prolactin, and this male, who was never interested in infants, will suddenly start to lick them, crouch over them, and retrieve them when they stray. One type of monkey, the marmoset, unlike other monkeys, makes a very devoted father. Indeed, the marmosets exhibit a high and significant correlation between prolactin and paternal behavior. In pigeons, males do suckle chicks with crop milk, and prolactin is responsible for both milk production and nurturing behavior.

When a mother gives birth, her level of prolactin is at its peak. If it fulfills its function and decomposes in body tissue, while directing the mother's actions toward the baby, creating maternal behavior, then the mother is happy. If the infant is taken from her, for example, in the event of death, and she is left with high prolactin with no one to give care to, she will sink into depression. Most mothers who have given birth feel slightly depressed, not in reaction to separation, but as an insignificant side effect of the increasing levels of prolactin. It passes quickly. Depression that is accompanied by crying ("third day crying") is a common event in maternity hospitals, and occurs in many mothers on the third day after they have given birth. This crying is accompanied by an abundant flow of milk. Both the crying and the plentiful milk are promoted by prolactin. Humans are one of the few creatures that cry emotionally with tears. The crocodile just emerges wet out of the water, and other creatures shed tears in response to an irritation, such as dust or wind. But emotional crying that is painful and sorrowful, with tears, is a very human phenomenon.

What is the connection between tears and emotions? Paul MacLean, the prominent American scientist, claimed that fire made the connection. Fire, a crucial evolutionary force tamed by humans about 2 million years ago, has been used since then to our advantage. Humans probably used to sit around the fire in the evening, perhaps in caves, to share experiences of togetherness, to tell heroic tales of the day, to fortify feelings of kinship and fraternity, to glory in another's victories, to share the pain and sorrow of someone's death. To this day we perform our festive and memorial ceremonies with fire: memorial candles, torches, and festive lights are commonly featured. The combination of fire with joy, empathy, and brotherhood, as well as with loss and pain at someone's death, was probably formed in the smoky caves. Smoke first brought tears of irritation to our eyes, and then, evolutionarily, tears became part of our emotional response. Natural selection has promoted both the attraction to fire and emotionality.

Empathy, identifying with one's fellow human in both better or worse times, brings tears to our eyes. When a proud athlete stands on the podium at the Olympic Games and cries at the sound of the national anthem and the sight of the flag (symbols of brotherhood), we shed tears with him. When we hear or watch a story of struggle and salvation, when Lassie returns home, or a foundling finds its mother, or an infant is saved from a predator, our eyes become moist with tears. And, of course, separation makes us weep. Saying farewell to our dead, a family member or a national leader who was murdered, brings tears to our eyes. The tribe shares tears of joy and tears of sorrow. Chemical analysis of tears reveals an astounding surprise: tears release prolactin. Surplus, depressive prolactin is created when we want to hug someone and there is no one to hug, when we have separated and there is no one on whom to focus the mother–child behavior. Women, as a group, have a basic higher level of prolactin in their serum than men, and they are more vulnerable to depression and crying. These are all components of motherhood, of sensitivity to bonding and of separation fear. Our culture's common perception of depression as a disorder is a sorry mistake. Depression has an important function, ensuring the enormous evolutionary achievements of relationship, unity, and love. Love could not have existed without its keeper, which warns us of a failure, thus bolstering our effort to fan the old flames.

EVOLUTION OF A LOVING BRAIN

As observed in the previous chapters, the talent and wish to love and be loved are products of natural selection, which shaped the human species for many generations and selected this ability. Evolution shaped all of life from the initial microorganism to appear on earth 4 billion years ago through fish that climbed out of the water and became reptiles and reptiles that claimed warm blood and became mammals to humans. Not all these species have a brain. The brain is a relatively new phenomenon, having started at some point in fish about half a billion years ago. The brain is essentially a supreme headquarters that takes on the supervision and control of the body through the nervous system. If love is indeed part of the evolutionary chain, then it is also supervised by the brain, and from our study of the brain's evolution, we should discover behaviors related to love.

Evolution is a chain of events that occur in organisms' DNA to change the next generation. One life form develops from its previous one. Every new form is a variation on the previous one, not a new creation, and the same goes for the brain. The supreme command of any newly adapted way of life is not a one-shot created brain but an accumulated brain, constructed of layer upon layer, whereas each new adaptation adds a course to the previous ones. Thus, the human brain of today can be viewed as an archeological dig in which chronological layers parallel the topographic continuum. The deeper the layer is within the brain, the more evolutionarily ancient it is, and the higher the layer, the more recent it is. If we were to "dig" into our brain, we would be digging through our evolution from the present time way into the past. The eminent brain researcher, Paul MacLean, spent a lifetime of work on understanding the evolutionary layered human brain amassed from fish to humans. He calls our brain the "Triune Brain" and says it is made of three major strata (see Figure 4).

The initial brain form was the advent of a crown in the central nervous system in fish. A slight thickening at the end of the spinal cord constitutes the "neural chassis" of the future brain. This marked the first appearance of central control, ruling the basic physiological functions. The chassis regulates metabolism, heart and blood system, digestion, respiration, and reproduction.

Now comes the first layer of the triune brain, which reptiles developed over the chassis. The reptiles added a number of structures composing what MacLean calls the reptilian complex. The striatal (reptilian) complex control in reptiles (and later in mammals and humans) the new behaviors that reptiles introduced into existing behavior repertoires.

An important behavior fostered by reptiles is territoriality. Reptiles value territoriality highly, marking their domain and guarding it meticulously through visual signals. They stand on the border of their property and nod their heads, seemingly signaling, "This is my territory."

The same reptilian brain is active in mammals and humans, and continues to control our territorial urge. And who better than we know how powerful

Figure 4
Human Layered Brain

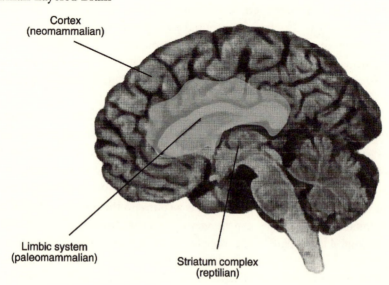

Cortex
(neomammalian)

Limbic system
(paleomammalian)

Striatum complex
(reptilian)

the urge to territoriality can be, and how horrible its consequences. Our world is continuously torn apart by cruel wars for tribal lands. Over and over, human groups are incited against each other to the death. One glance at the map of what used to be Yugoslavia, or the USSR, or Somalia, or Rwanda will suffice to understand that we are all fiercely involved in territoriality. These wars are sometimes absurd: populations who had lived together in harmony for gen-erations are suddenly full of hatred and fury, and when the battles cease they can again live side by side in peace. We know that the fighting was senseless, but it was ignited by that zealous brain infrastructure, which furiously fights over territory and which, when ignited by circumstance, will burn away despite its irrational aspects. And why look far? In Israel, territoriality has been shaking every person and every government for the past 100 years. This fierce archaic force, which drives people to speak about sacred land, to kiss it, to worship its rocks, stems from the depths of the reptilian brain.

The force of territoriality can also be found in humans on an individual rather than a group level. We would not enter another's home without knocking on the door or ringing the doorbell, and would enter only if permission were granted. The feeling that we are not to invade another's territory is deeply embedded in us. Whoever is caught entering someone else's territory will surely be taken to one of two places: jail or a lunatic asylum.

An additional and very important behavior controlled by the reptilian brain is everyday life, routines and subroutines. Reptiles are such creatures of habit that we could set a clock by their daily conduct. They get up at the same time every morning, say 5 A.M., and go to the exact same place to bask in the sun. They then go to the same place at the exact time to relieve themselves and to the same place to drink water every day at the same hour. They then forage in their close vicinity and take their compulsory afternoon nap. Next they go foraging a little further from home, and finally, at precisely 5:30 in the evening, each returns to exactly its own place for sleep. Some subroutines can be inserted into this routine.

Paul MacLean reports an interesting example: a group of lizards, whose territory was the roof of a barn, acted according to all the daily rules, and at the end of the day would return to their sleeping place on the barn roof. The researcher was amazed to see that instead of taking the easy route to the roof, night after night the lizards chose a much more difficult course on a diagonal plank from the ground to the rooftop. The plank was at such an angle that the lizards found it very hard to climb, and sometimes fell down. Yet they would persistently try to climb up the plank rather than take the easier way. Appar-ently, the explanation is the sacred precedent; reptiles are even fonder of precedents than lawyers. It can be assumed that once long ago some ancient forefathers preferred the difficult route to the easy one (perhaps there was a puddle or perhaps a cat), and ever since they have been repeating the same route because a precedent ensures success. If it succeeded once, it will succeed again. This is the powerful motivation for recurring routines.

This reflects our passion for habits. We find it extremely difficult to abandon our habits, for they are strongly rooted in the depths of our brains. When this need works overtime, we have compulsive behavior in which we rigidly repeat the same actions over and over again. The obsessive-compulsive disorder is motivated by a strong anxiety, which is relieved to some degree by reenacting a ritual: the familiar route is the safest. Obeying the same procedure again and again ensures a sort of homing. When studying the psychological feeling of these people, we get the same answer: it affords a feeling of security. From an evolutionary point of view, this makes sense, for if something succeeded once, the probability of it succeeding again is higher, and the feeling of security and the wish to reproduce the same action again rise.

Obviously, compulsive behavior is an extreme dose of the basic principle, but the principle itself is correct, being healthy and wired in every brain. It enables orientation in the environment and the performance of routine actions of any animal, after it has learned the details relevant to its lifestyle. If it learned the path that leads to water, it will repeat it because the water is really there. Territoriality, the first passion of reptiles, is aided by their desire for routines. So are social behaviors, establishing status hierarchy, courtship dances, and any other everyday handling of survival missions in the minefield of life, by using the "correct" secured path. Why risk a new one?

The inclination to routinely reproduce the same action is also apparent in visual communication. The lizard nodding its head is saying something symbolic: "This is me, and this is my importance," or "This is my territory." We can find similar behavior in any army camp, where many people raise their hands in salute. This action symbolizes something: this is me, this is my importance or my rank, referring to someone else's rank. The combination of repeating the same action with its symbolic significance leads to ritual. Our lives are full of rituals. Watch a basketball player at the penalty line, getting ready to score the crucial points of the game. He repeats the same ritual over and over: he bounces the ball twice, or he spits on his hands and rubs them together, or he practices a "dry run" of his forthcoming throw. This carries on to larger ceremonies and our holidays, which are conducted according to preordained rules that are not to be overstepped. Every holiday has its food, blessings, songs, gifts, lights, even the seating of the guests, which are repeated immutably every year. All rites are rituals, which we reproduce over and over again at given intervals—the same commandment at the same hour, the same reading of the same portion of the Bible the same week, the same prayer every morning and a different same one every evening, this one on Sunday and a different one on weekdays. Overstepping the rules is dangerous. We like the repetitiveness and symbolism of ceremonies because they give us a sense of security. This ancient sense of security lies deep in the recesses of evolutionary time and of our brains, and therein lies its strength.

Mammals added the "limbic system" to the reptilian complex. This is the second layer of the triune brain, and is the contribution of the emotional creatures, the warm-blooded mammals. Our emotions are processed in the limbic system, a collection of cerebral structures around the brain stem. The limbic system allows us to feel, to empathize, and to love. We could not love if it weren't for the limbic system.

The limbic system is connected by many neural pathways to the brain stem and the neural chassis—that is, to the areas that control our basic physiological functions, and this is how the familiar link between emotional and physical excitement is made. The Gordian knot holding together emotional excitement and body-heat maintaining physiology is especially interesting. Since mammals who invented the preservation of body heat by evolving special mechanisms also invented emotionality by use of the same means (hormones, for instance), we get a "superfluous" reaction of heat regulation mechanisms when we become excited. The combination of warm feelings in a body that has warm blood creates well-known phenomena—shivers (from fear or joy), blushing, paleness, "goose-bumps," perspiration—all mechanisms that are intended to supervise body heat and appear as a byproduct of excitement.

Yet another fascinating association exists between the physiology of metabolism and excitement. Metabolism is essentially a matter of bringing something in and extracting something. Here emotions come, and when we love and are full of positive feelings, we express it by "bringing in." "I'll gobble you up," is what we say to a sweet baby. We want to kiss, to hug someone we like, to absorb the loved one. On the other hand, negative feelings are expressed by "extracting": sticking out the tongue, spitting, and so on. Emotionality can, therefore, be regarded as yet another layer of the brain's dealing with reality, with one more device of information processing and interpreting.

The primitive ancient brain brings in and extracts with indifference, whereas the new brain grants it negative or positive added-value. The sophisticated, sensitive mammal recognizes good and bad, with emotions that prompted it to bring in the good and loved, and to put out the bad and hated. There is no neutral emotionality: it judges the world, and it empowers reactions towards it. Emotionality is what mammal mothers introduced over the functionalistic earlier parenthood. If we were to deliberately damage the limbic system of pregnant monkeys, we would cancel their maternal feelings. Pregnant monkeys whose limbic system has been demolished will give birth but will pay no attention to their offspring, as if we set them back millions of evolution years and turned them into unresponsive reptilian mothers. If the limbic system of infant apes is injured, their ability to call out to their mothers is neutralized. Again, this call to mother is emotional excitement, which each and every one of us knows either as separation fear or as the joy of reunion.

Of which matter did evolution create these new emotional layers and emotional functioning? Some of the most important matters in the emotional game are hormones. Prior to the mammals, hormones controlled maternal physiology (just as they control many other events in the body), duties related to reproduction, ovulation, and egg-laying. By means of accumulating significant mutations, which were selected for giving an advantage in the parental-emotional milieu, maternal hormones started to link ancient physiological functions with the new excitement, indulgence, enthusiasm, and devotion. Thus, reproduction has turned into an emotionally charged process by putting indifferent hormones and basic physiology to new uses and by constructing new brain areas and new neural tracks.

The new hormonal-neural style can be detected when it does futile work, as in radical mood swings during a woman's menstruation period or menopause. Menstruation and menopause are highlights of emotionality only because the related hormonal changes generate, as a futile byproduct, extreme moods. Menopause and menstruation are well known to involve depression and anxiety. The aim of anxiety is to better guard the infant, and the goal of depression is to avoid separation. The production of both in the brain is hormone-dependent.

Within the limbic system, one of the areas motherhood claims is the cingulate cortex. Recently, this area has been found to be rich in opiate receptors. The brain produces endorphins, morphinelike matter, that affects the brain much like opium. Endorphins give a feeling of a "high," inducing a sense of well-being, relaxation, satisfaction, and pleasure. Since the cingulate cortex is so closely related to motherhood, we can assume that when the mother performs a motherly action, such as feeding, protecting, and caring for the infant's welfare, she is rewarded by endorphins. As a result, she feels joy and satisfaction and a euphoria much as if she were on a "trip." Pleasure and satisfaction are the prizes that evolution has selected to reward "correct" actions. Endorphins are a matter of pleasure.

The third and last layer in the evolution of the brain is the new cortex, which was added by the later mammals. Humans worked wonders in this area. In the human brain, the new cortex takes up about 80% of total brain volume, and therein lies the human's preeminence, notably, the ability to use words and other languages, the language of computers or music or mathematics; the ability to think logically and to learn rules; the sophisticated ability to measure space and time. No other living creature can make a lover's date for any time, at any place on earth—and keep it. And there lie morals and conscience, which are the verbal, somewhat dry level of knowing what emotionality feels, of good and bad. A conscience can "feel" happy or pricked. Conscience feels because the new cortex is connected to the old limbic system, and the performance of a moral action is emotionally prompted on the one hand and emotionally rewarded on the other. Just as the limbic system adds a layer for emotional treatment of reality, so the new cortex adds another layer for deciphering the world around us, by means of words, concepts and symbols, laws and logic—the peak of which is rationality.

The three brains act in harmony and reciprocity, nourishing each other and activating each other. Nevertheless, each has its own special features, and each paints behavior in different characterizations and qualities. Human loving behavior relies on a mixture of influences derived from each layer. "Reptile love," or rather reptile relationship, is very down to earth, functional, and blunt, whereas limbic love is excited and enthusiastic and cortical love reasoned.

8

THE HIERARCHY OF LOVE
STYLES IN THE BRAIN

Since every evolutionary era bequeathed a different behavior style built into our brains, we might find ourselves in conflicting situations in many areas of our lives. For instance, with regard to maternal behavior, will we be a mother lizard who lays her eggs and goes out for a good time, or will we be a breast-feeding, eager mother, or perhaps a speaking, rational mother concerned about her child's school report? Someone must instill some order into these conflicting forces. One mother cannot be both indifferent and enthusiastic at the same time, at once hysterical and reasonable. She is one person combining three mothers. How will she act? Evolutionary logic states that order must be instilled hierarchically, from new to old. New ought to be preferred to old; otherwise there would be no evolution. If the enthusiastic mother does not subdue the indifferent one, we will have no devoted motherhood. If the sensible mother does not subdue the sensitive one, the child will not benefit from human preeminence. Some sort of ordered hierarchy evolved wherein the cortex bends the limbic and the limbic bends the reptilian brain. The new behavior, the latest word in evolution, gains priority. How can this rule be carried into practice?

We could imagine a kind of suppression mechanism that descends through sophisticated neural pathways from top to bottom. We must remember, however, that this is a suppressing, not an annihilating mechanism, because ancient parts of the brain are essential. The ancient deals with the basic physiological foundations of our lives. The reptilian brain supervises everyday routines, and we would not find our way around without it. The limbic system enables us to feel, to evaluate good and bad, and to love. This region enables loving motherhood. If the cortex were to tyrannically destroy all of this, where would we be?

As an illustration of this idea, let us look at the Israeli kibbutz in its early days. The kibbutz was established as a new social way of life that would raise a "new kind of human" by means of an ideological, educated, and enlightened rationality. This "cortical" approach promoted the repression of "limbic" motherhood, of the tenderness, warmth, and physical proximity between mother and offspring. Mothers in the old kibbutz were forced to waive joint residence with their children. Babies were given to communal children-houses to get a proper education. Most of the care—feeding, dressing, cleaning, playing, and education—were in the hands of an appointed minder, and for most hours of the day mothers were even forbidden to visit their children. In some cases, the mother of a sick child was not allowed to approach its bed. The child "spent" two to three hours a day with its parents, but even then the universal motherly hug, clasping the child to the mother's bosom, was prohibited by educational edict, because that would "spoil" the child. Ultimately, this inanity was rectified, and expressions of tenderness and warm feelings were reinstated. Emotionality triumphed in the end because the brain's mechanism of repression had no choice but to maintain the previous, vital area. Thus, today emotionality is alive and kicking in kibbutz mothers. The brain is therefore ambivalent. It treats the lower area as if they had few rights; but still essential, they are the indispensable hewers of wood and drawers of water one needs but disdains.

Since evolution preserves the ancient brain layers, albeit suppressed, they still exist, bustling with activity and energy, despite repression. As with any other live organism when subjugated, individual or nation, imprisoned or occupied, will seek loopholes that make self-realization possible. When the suppression mechanism is sleepy, they find their opportunity, just as in guerrilla warfare. Indeed, the outbursts of the deep brain layers occur when repression is weakened, and enable us a glimpse into the evolutionary depths of our brains. Dreams, for instance, offer us a glance into our evolutionary depths. Dreams are supervised not by the rational, logical, speaking, cortical mentality, but by a world of emotions and images, unaware of logic and physics rules. That is why dreams are weird. Drunkenness is also a chance to look at secrets, which are normally controlled by the cortex, for *in vino veritas*. Drugs, too, activate lower brain areas and reduce the control performed by our severe censor, the cortex.

Mental disorders could be explained as overactivity or imbalance of lower brain areas. Paranoia, for instance, which is an attack of fierce fright, stems from unsupervised activity of the amygdala, an important part of the emotional limbic system. The amygdala is responsible for a creature's ability to experience fear, one of the talents that is most crucial to its survival. But if this ability works overtime, humans go crazy with fear, and that is the essence of paranoia. An especially good example is obsessive-compulsive behavior. In this case, the reptilian complex is hard at work. Compulsive people feel the need to repeat, check, and ensure things. They walk the street and count poles; they can stand for hours in front of the refrigerator to check if the light actually goes out when the door closes; they wash themselves or their homes a hundred times a day to make sure there is no dirt in the vicinity. The primitive reptilian structure tends to repeat itself, stereotypically and almost automatically, in obedience to rules that were learned and wired into the neural circuits in a persistently repetitive pattern. Since it is an ancient brain, it is dominated by the higher, more flexible brain areas.

Establishing dominance takes time, however, and children, during their development, give us a chance to observe the process as it happens in front of our eyes. Children from the ages of 4 to 10 are a bit compulsive in both behavior and thoughts, in a way that is reminiscent of obsessive-compulsive illness. At around the age of 4 to 5, we can notice behaviors such as "I mustn't step on the cracks in the sidewalk, or I'll die," or "If I count all the poles on the way to school, it will stop raining," or "I have to repeat the same ritual every night before I go to bed, so I don't have bad dreams." Later on, when the repression mechanism, activated by the higher cortex on the lower reptilian brain, ripens and matures, the child is released from reptilian rigidity and can adopt more flexible and intelligent behavior. If struck by a car, or some illness, or an oppressive stress, however, then all of a sudden compulsiveness will return. The disaster will weaken the repression of the new brain over the old one.

Reflexes are similar. For instance, at birth every infant is checked for the Babinsky reflex. This reflex, which indicates normality, is exhibited when the baby's sole is tickled; the result is a typical bending of the toes and protrusion of the big toe. This reflex is present in all infants, it is a sign of health, and it disappears at 18 months. It does not actually disappear, but it is merely restricted. If the toddler, the child, or the adult is involved in an accident and severely injures its nape and spinal chord, the Babinsky reflex might reappear but this time it would be an ill omen. It would be a sign that the neural cable, leading from the upper brain area to dominate the reflexivity of the lower nervous system, was severed. Just as the Babinsky reflex is healthy in an infant and will reappear in adults only in case of damage disconnecting the repression mechanism, so does compulsive behavior—normal in children—vanish and show up again in adults only in case of brain hierarchy malfunctioning. As a primitive method of orientation, compulsive behavior is good. It is under control in more intelligent creatures. The repression mechanism favors new over old, but does not eradicate the ancient behavior styles. The Babinsky reflex is either there or not there; there are only these two possibilities. Compulsiveness is spread over a continuum. Some of it stems continuously from the reptilian brain, for our own good. Dosage is the important variable.

Brain hierarchy is also recognized in styles of love relationships between men and women. The reptilian brain pushes humans towards a blunt and functionalist sexual connection, a coming together of genitals rather than of hearts. This type of relationship involves much forcefulness and violence. In many species, both reptiles and mammals, sex and aggression go hand in hand. The male takes the female, subdues her, and does the deed, in many cases biting her neck and hurting her to the point of drawing blood. In humane-moral terms, this would be considered abuse and degradation. Still, to a smaller or larger extent, sexuality of this type is present in the depths of our brains.

The limbic brain is essentially different, conducting an excited, rutting love relationship in which hormones flood the brain stormily and enthusiastically, and cause feelings of bewilderment to the point of clouded consciousness and mindlessness. We know who we have fallen in love with, but we find it very hard to explain why because the source of blinding, sweeping love is the nonverbal limbic system, which is emotional and sentimental but lacks words and cannot elucidate things. The human cortex leads to a new kind of relationship that is unique to humans and an important element of human preeminence, the kind that makes marriage and family possible. It encourages a permanent, long-term bonding that gives preference to considerations of children's welfare, finances, family, and social connections over hormonal excitement. Therefore, cortical love is much less excitable. It is emotionally moderate, and it combines new moral values, unknown to previous evolutionary generations, such as mutual aid, mutual respect, partnership, and sometimes even equality between the sexes.

In order to enable the evolution of the family, which represents one of the most momentous human phenomena, brain hierarchy had to give preference to the cortex over the limbic and reptilian brains. But, as already stated, the repressed continue living and seek assertion. One way to assert themselves is through dreams. A woman's dream from the Bible, Song of Songs 5, offers an orderly, gradual procession of first cortical, then limbic, and finally reptilian expression of the brain, and allows us to perceive the three brain qualities which are so different.

The first declaration informs us that she is dreaming: "I sleep, but my heart is awake." She then hears the voice of her lover. Notice the words he uses: lofty, valiant, equal, beautiful—cortical words: "Open to me, my sister, my love, my dove, my undefiled; for my head is filled with dew, my locks with the drops of the night." Her answer is also extremely rational, cortical: "I have put off my coat, how shall I put it on? I have washed my feet, how shall I defile them?" Then comes the descent. Words disappear, to be replaced by excitement. We have moved from the cortex to the limbic: "My beloved stretched forth his hand through the opening, and my inmost parts were moved for him. I rose to open up to my beloved, and my hands dropped with myrrh, and my fingers with flowing myrrh upon the handles of the lock." No words, just lots of fluids. Now we sink one more step into the forceful, violent, abusive, degrading reptilian brain. "I opened to my beloved, but my beloved had turned away and was gone. My soul failed me when he spoke. I sought him, but I could not find him; I called him, but he gave me no answer. The watchmen that go about the city found me, they smote me, they wounded me; the keepers of the walls took away my mantle from me." This seems to be a scene of sexual violence, group rape. At the frightening end, she awakens and is confronted with an uncomfortable feeling, awareness of what she dreamed, and she says: "I adjure you, O daughters of Jerusalem, if you find my beloved, what will you tell him? That I am love-sick."

Knowledge that these occurrences happen in and to me leads to severe guilt: I am sick. If I can dream that I am beaten, raped, and my mantle is taken away, then something in me is sick. Unfortunately, many psychologists would give their female patients the same guilt-feeling when analyzing such a dream. The sense of being sick is a reaction of the cortex. The upper cortex, which prefers love in which "my sister, my love" is "my dove, my undefiled," is the one that shames and scolds us when we stoop low and pour out our fluids, or when we stoop even lower and combine sex with violence. In its critical opinion we are not okay. That is the cortex's way of obtaining obedience by means of condemnation and guilt. That very cortex blinds the doctrine of psychologists and therapists.

The existence of varied-quality brain areas, and the need to express each quality, on the one hand, and to prefer each over the other, on the other hand, require a constant striving for balance. The brain hierarchy that gives preference to the cortex over the limbic and to the limbic over the reptilian brain has a parallel hierarchy in our value system, by which we tend to prefer the rational, reasoned action to the lower urges. When we are consulted on matters of love, or on any other subject for that matter, we advise following the head rather than the heart. When a friend comes to us all upset and tells us about a big argument, and says excitedly "I'll get a divorce" or "I'll resign," we usually say: "Wait, count to ten, sleep on it." In other words, we suggest that the cortex be given enough time to take control, and then the discussion of whether or not to divorce or whether or not to resign will be a better one.

Rational, cortical preference is indubitably highly important and can produce reasonable decisions. But it should be stressed that the cortex is new in an evolutionary sense. The human cortex is only a few million years old. On the other hand, the emotional limbic system is a wise, experienced old lady, and has been rooted in the mammalian brain for 100 to 150 million years. It has accumulated a lot of insights and possesses fine-tuned and observant senses. The cortex is indeed inflated and has an inflated ego. It thinks highly of itself and so do we, but it is only a weanling. If we were to look closely at decisions we make, we might find that rather than guiding us to rational decisions, the cortex specializes in rationalizations after the deed. The intuitive, gut-feeling limbic determines a great deal in our decisions; the cortex, in its self-importance, then comes along to rationalize, reason, and explain in pretty words.

The extent of the importance of healthy balance within the brain can be seen in various types of marriages. Matches with a strong emphasis on the reptilian brain are tough, cold marriages. There is sex, but there is neither intimacy nor caring. On the contrary, when the limbic system is dominant, the salient feature will be excitable falling-in-love, which like oestrus, passes. Falling in love anew will happen over and over again. It is doubtful whether such a union can last. Marriages in which the major emphasis is on the cortex would be dry, like accounting, in which loss and gain are the central issue. All warmth, emotion, and tenderness would be missing. The same goes for every area of life. We have in us conflicting forces, which must be expressed in a balanced way. If we carefully handle each one of these conflicting forces in a balanced fashion, we will be contributing more to our own mental health, and to achieving a better sex and love life than those who would stress this or that quality, while depriving the others.

THE HIERARCHY OF SEXUAL STYLES IN THE BRAIN

The brain, as we have stated, is the supreme headquarters of behavior. When evolution selects a new adaptation in a new species, it is governed by supplements and innovations to the brain. The additions are composed of neural cell layers, one over the other. A new layer is connected to an old one by many neural fibers and has a reciprocal relationship with it.

On the central axis of the brain an ancient, primitive path conveys input from the once dominant sense—the sense of smell. The olfactory bulb is located in the frontal lobe, and a great number of neural pathways radiate from it to various brain areas. The olfactory bulb has been significant throughout evolution. It is easy to notice that a dog, for instance, runs its life by smell. Its nose dictates what to eat and with whom to mate. A great number of creatures, prior to humans on the evolutionary chain, act just the same.

The close connection between scent and behavior is built into the spinal chord, in the brain stem, and then into the limbic system. The loosening of its interdependence occurred only in the new cortex, and mainly the brand-new cortex of apes and humans, who greatly developed sight and began to rely less on scent and more on vision. When we want to decide what to eat, we look at it first, similarly, when we want to decide who to mate with, we look first. Still we also lend some importance to smell; it is meaningful in food and probably in sexuality as well. Indirect evidence that scent does play a role in human sexuality is the synchronization of the menstruation cycles in women who live in the same house for a number of months. For instance, a coed from the South and a coed from the North, whose cycles are on different dates and who room together on campus, might find that within a few months they will ovulate and get their periods at the same time. The same phenomenon happens to mothers and daughters, who live together. This synchronization is probably controlled by pheromones, scent particles distributed by the reproductive system, which played a crucial role in ancient sexuality.

Without doubt, however, our brain hierarchy prefers the visual to the olfactory system. Nevertheless, the ancient brain still exists and is an essential condition of sexual activity. According to the brain hierarchy principles, new functions are awarded preference, but the old ones are still alive and kicking. This duality might cast new light on a number of problematic issues of human sexuality. Let us begin with infants.

Most mothers of baby boys have witnessed the slightly embarrassing phenomenon that the baby gets an erection while suckling. Even Freud, however, would not have attributed this to the Oedipal complex. The male infant is not sexually attracted to its mother. This phenomenon is only ancient innervation, and is not yet overruled by the new cortex. The olfactory bulb, by means of abundant neural fibers, leads from the frontal lobe to the lower area of the limbic system, where the amygdala is located. The amygdala is an important center of oral behavior—of the mouth and eating. (Smell is used to determine what was eaten.) The olfactory information also flows through rich neural extensions to the upper area of the limbic system to the septum, which is an important center of sexual behavior. (Smell used to determine who one mated with.) The septum and amygdala are interconnected by a wide neural highway (see Figure 5). The baby smells its mother while suckling, and then all the neural network connections of the olfactory innervations, the amygdala, and the septum "turn each other on" in a process that is somewhat similar to electric induction. The infant suckles, and his sexual system responds with an erection. After a number of months, the brain is upgraded, and the cortex builds up its ability to repress lower areas, just as it represses atavistic reflexes in infants. The baby will then eat three meals a day without getting an erection. Growing up, the young man will enter sexual relations, including oral sex; that is, he will again use his mouth in a sexual way.

Although the moral, enlightened cortex does not especially advocate oral sex, if we were to ask married couples in the United States, we would find that about 95% perform oral sex. Why do they need their mouths if they have genitals? The answer they give to this question is simple: it is more stimulating, more enjoyable. And why is that so? Because with some simplification we can say that the levels of stimulation and excitement are actually the product of the quantity of neurons turned on during sexual activity. The more neurons turned

Figure 5
Oral and Aggressive Sexuality in the Human Brain

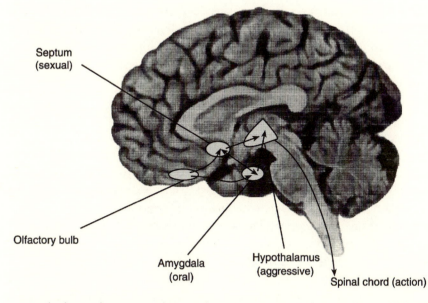

Septum (sexual)

Olfactory bulb

Amygdala (oral)

Hypothalamus (aggressive)

Spinal chord (action)

on in the brain during copulation, the more arousing, the sexual act will be. If we add the mouth to sexuality, we proceed to increase the quantity of turned-on neurons. To the cells that innervate the septum via the brain stem to the genitals we also add the cells innervating the amygdala to the septum and the amygdala to the brain stem and the genitals. One gains more electrified neurons and thus also gains heightened sexual pleasure. This trick is powered by the ancient brain infrastructure, which is still alive and well.

Oral sex harms no one, but the ancient structure of sexuality creates an additional phenomenon, which is much more problematic. In many creatures the behaviors supervised by the sense of smell—eating and sex—are connected to aggression. They fight over food and they fight over females. Therefore, the brain is designed in such a way that both the amygdala, which supervises oral eating behavior, and the septum, which is in charge of sexual behavior, send out neural extensions that converge in the brain stem, in an area called the hypothalamus, and it fiercely blows an aura of militant aggression onto them. When sexuality becomes aggressive, an ancient creature will be triumphant, but we of the moral cortex have serious problems. When a monkey stands on the border of its territory and faces an invader, it is full of aggression, and due to the neural networks in the brain, an erection and chewing motions will also be evident. After this monkey has been guarding its territory for a multitude of evolutionary generations with an erection, then the erection becomes a signal, a language understood by any invader. The erection says: "Beware of me! I am strong and dangerous and I will attack you." When a strange monkey encounters an erect penis, it immediately understands the ramifications. The ability to interpret the significance of an erection was selected by evolution. Ancient monkeys, who did not comprehend the hint and were not careful, were attacked and killed, and hence they are not our ancestors. Only monkeys who understood this reproduced and bequeathed the new perception to their offspring.

This symbolism is clear today to monkeys, apes, and humans, even if they didn't go to school. You might try to go out during rush-hour traffic and watch angry drivers, sticking out their finger to form a male organ as a gesture of angry aggression. The so common use of expressions that includes "fuck" is actually a verbal equalization of a sexual act to a damaging act. Such an expression is an unmistakable combination of aggressive sexuality, in which the penis is used as a weapon. The success of these gestures and expressions in modern life stems from the fact that all of us, in the depths of our brains, perfectly understand the link between sexuality and aggression. The link is wired there deeply.

The upper cortex attempts to control aggressive sexuality and instead suggests lofty ideals: honor, equality, tenderness, and grace. But we must keep in mind that sexual excitement and orgasm cannot avoid passage through the central pathway of the brain stem. There is no orgasm in the cortex. Orgasms are supervised from the brain stem to the genitals, and therefore if people do not want to give up orgasms, they must avail themselves of the lower brain areas activating. Only the pretty words of the Song of Songs can keep it all dry. Rationality without sensuality, reasoning without passion, cannot generate excitement and satisfaction. Sensuality and passion are innervated in the lower brain areas, and they must be stimulated. This is the reason for the sweeping popularity of pornography, which has become a million dollar industry. Pornography is designed to appeal mainly to men who may have a wife at home with whom they have a respectful and mutual relationship. Still they sneak off during their lunch break to a dark movie house to watch blunt, violent, barren, loveless sex. Pornography gives voice to ancient, but still essential, sexual styles subdued by cortical love.

This is also the reason for an even more frequent phenomenon. The number of men and women who have sexual fantasies is much larger than the number of pornography consumers. Fantasies are not the sole domain of lonely people, who have no sexual partner, and therefore fantasize and masturbate. All of us, even the married among us who sleep regularly with a mate, incorporate fantasies into the sexual act. What is the content of the fantasy? It is not of some innocent siesta in a hammock on a Pacific island, coconut palms swaying above and white sand beneath. No, the fantasy is one of forcefulness, at times of violence, even to a degree of pain and humiliation. Sadomasochism, which is a form of sexuality that takes pain and humiliation to its extreme, is an example of the radical use of the ancient brain. To some, the voice of ancient brain layers, the practice of forceful sexuality is so extreme that sadomasochism becomes their only way to enjoy sex. But it is only a question of dosage. Any one of us can feel something of sadomasochism; but most of us, fortunately, make do with only fantasies.

Fetishism, which is the utilization of some object in order to reach sexual stimulation and orgasm, such as a girl's red panties is also based on the rules of ancient brain innervation. As you will recall, the reptilian brain creates closed neural circuits that repeat the same stereotypic behavior over and over. After relevant information is received from the environment at the beginning of their life, it will show up again and again automatically. The female turtle will return to lay her eggs at the exact same spot on the same beach where she herself hatched. If that rigid pattern endangers her life, for instance, if a highway has now been built on the spot, she will steadfastly march to her death. Closure of the behavior cycle is more powerful than any other judgment. This is how full behavior is built around a first "sign"—courting around the scent of spring, nesting around the fall of leaves, going to sleep around sunset. And if the sign appears, the entire behavior web will be completed.

When a person is locked on a certain fetish and cannot reach orgasm in any other way, it might be due to strong "soldering" of the ancient brain neural circuit, which is activated by a "sign-stimulant" and ends in orgasm. This circuit was wired, just as in an ancient creature. There is a famous example of an epileptic, who could reach orgasm at any time by holding a safety pin in front of his eyes. Unfortunately, he could not do it with a woman. He did not love the safety pin, but he had sexual intercourse with it via his ancient brain, which holds no capacity for feelings and love, and still controls orgasms. The cortex does not like low sexuality and tries to suppress it. And as is the wont of suppressers, it delegitimizes the submissive elements. "That's not nice," it tells us, "That's dirty." We are left with the dilemma of either forgoing powerful stimulation and even orgasm or of feeling guilty. The safe way out of this imbroglio is not simple and perhaps does not even exist. We must learn to live with contradictions, to keep our dirty fantasies privately to ourselves, and not to express them openly.

This is the least we could deduce from the bitter experience of the two heroes, Ilana and Alexander, in Amos Oz's wonderful book *Black Box*. The book tries to decipher the reasons for why their marriage failed, as recorded in the black box. The deciphering vehicle is the correspondence between them, in which they describe the process they underwent. The letters reveal that from the beginning of their relationship, the couple greatly stressed the reptilian brain aspects. Ilana writes to Alexander Gideon, her ex-husband, about the moment she was first attracted to him. He was a regimental commander in the army, and she was his clerk. This is the classic order of strong conqueror versus his subordinate. And so she writes:

> as if enchanted, from the troubled depths of ancient feminine servility, was I attracted to you. Old-days slavery, before words existed. Surrender of a Neanderthal female, whose blinded survival sense, along with the horror of famine and chill, dropped her at the feet of the cruelest hunter, the hairy savage, who will bind her hands behind her back and carry his booty to his cave.

That was how it started, and that was how it continued. After they were married, and Alexander spent the whole work week away in the army, Ilana led a totally reptilian sex life in their home in Jerusalem. She used to pick up dirty, wretched, pitiful men, take them home with her, and let them have intercourse with her. When Alexander came home for the weekend, she would tell him about her exploits. Blinded with fury, he would beat her and rape her, to both their pain and pleasure. Reptilian sex life of this kind does not sit well with the cortical essence of humans, not even with the limbic one. Both Ilana and Alex definitely had cortical and limbic values. Alas, they could not curb their archaic drives to the optimal level, and that is why their marriage failed.

Balance between lower sexual areas of the brain and the lofty upper areas is vital. There would be no pleasure without the lower area, and there would be no beautiful moral, humane feeling without the upper. How is this done? The solution perhaps, lies in the combination of hidden, unrealized fantasy, of which there is no need to speak and which enhances excitement, together with open, cortical, human behavior, which provides us with the feeling that we are moral humans who love ourselves and can thus lead long-term family lives.

The "triune brain," as studied, researched, and written about by Paul MacLean with such assiduousness and wisdom, consists of much more than a triple-component system. Evolution of the brain is not just in three stages but through a rich continuum of deposits left by a long chain of creatures, who displayed different and varied behavior styles. The relations within the brain consist of many more rich subtleties and intricacies than just the mutual influences between the brain stem, limbic system, and cortex, and each of the three is built of many separate regions. We must be wary of the over simplistic observations employed in order to analyze the brain strata in the last three chapters. It is much more complex than A, B, C. In justification, we should emphasize that the sin of simplicity is a necessity if we wish to derive laws in order to explain phenomena and to make some sense of a world that supplies us with an infinite number of variations. Yes, I have oversimplified, but on the other hand, I would like to urge the reader to constantly remember that life is much more complex than any statement we presume to make about it.

10

EVOLUTION OF SEXUALITY

Evolution progressed largely without sexuality. Of the 4 billion years of life on earth, sexuality emerged only in the last billion. Its prevalence raises uneasy and unsolved questions because natural selection selects whatever succeeds in the transmission of genes to subsequent generations. If a child could be produced alone, evolution would just love the producers who manage to replicate the whole of themselves in their offspring. A single parent therefore passes on his entire self, and the offspring is a genetic copy. When there are two parents, they share the "profits," and the child is 50% father and 50% mother, not to mention all the heartache, disappointments, valuable time, or money involved in bringing two parents together. How might we explain this? How was sexuality selected over the more profitable reproduction, and why is it prospering?

One answer lies in the advantages offered by variance. When there are two genetic sources in one offspring, it is a variation. It is not the father or the mother, but a new, as yet unknown variation. Variations, by their very nature, are inquisitive, flexible, adaptable to new conditions, and bold. If the need emerges to rise from the ocean to dry land, a great deal of variance is required; if a need arises to adapt to the ice age, a great deal of variance is needed; if there is a sudden transfer from forest to savanna, a great deal of variance is called for. Sexuality offers a lot of variance. As was mentioned in Chapter 2, William Hamilton, the bold Oxford biologist, emphasizes the necessity of variance for the immunization arms race. Our life is, to a great extent, a constant battle with small, invisible enemies: viruses, microbes, germs. This battle is like a neck-to-neck race of innovations. As all drug manufacturers know, viruses and germs renew themselves constantly, and our antibodies must adjust at a frightening pace. Change requires genetic variance, and when two parents contribute their genes to the immune system, the offspring is all the more abundant.

In order to illustrate how two parents increase the variance in their children, let us do some arithmetic. Every person has about 100,000 genes, and each gene has a parallel gene on a dual chromosome. Of the 100,000 genes, approximately 6.7% do not have an identical parallel gene, but different, meaning that there is 6.7% of variance within every human. Of every pair of parallel genes, the parent transmits one of two; the choice between the two is random. If so, every parent can produce 2 by the power of 6,700 various sex cells. This number can be translated into 10^{2017}, which is indeed a huge number. In order to illustrate the size of this figure, aided by a comparison, note that the number of all known atoms in the entire universe is 10^{80}. Thus, two parents can produce an infinite number of variations of children. But still two parents do not have to be of two different sexes. We could imagine two parents, each with different genes but not different genders—just two people. Then the pool of possible mates would be much bigger. One would not have to choose out of only 50% of the population, but anyone who wasn't oneself. This method does exist in some primitive creatures, such as fungi. Why not all the rest? The answer to this question is even more complex.

There are no agreed-upon solutions. One of the best suggestions is one propounded by the biologists Parker, Baker, and Smith, and it claims that at first there really were equal parents and equal sex cells. There were no spermatozoa versus ovum, just uniform gametes. Every living creature would release one sex cell into the water, or any other meeting place, and two gametes—two sex cells—would meet and create a new offspring. As in any phenomenon, gametes are not absolutely identical to each other. There is a distribution around the average. Some are small, by chance, and some are large, by chance. From the point of view of the offspring's chances to succeed, the larger has an advantage because it offers the fetus a lot of provisions. Therefore, the big gametes are preferable; they have many "suitors." In evolution, fat is beautiful, so that a bigger and fatter gamete will be chosen. But who will manage to grab the fat gamete? The agile one. And which one is agile? The little one. The smaller it is, the faster it is, and the faster it is, it will catch a fatter one, thus ensuring its offspring more "sandwiches to go."

From a random, meaningless start, which derives from random distribution around the average, we have two separate evolutionary paths. One selects a fatter and fatter gamete, which reproduces fatter and fatter gametes, and the other selects smaller and quicker gametes, which reproduce even smaller and faster gametes. This is actually evolution as a principle. From some starting point, which could be casual, phenomena evolve one after the other, and natural selection amplifies advantageous features that are more and more to the nonreturn point: be big or be small. If mediocre, you will not be able to stand your ground before your enemies. The fat gamete develops an honest strategy; it offers everything it can. The little gamete, on the other hand, acquires an exploitative strategy; it takes advantage of the fat one's donation. Furthermore, when semen aspires to be even smaller and its aim is to transmit nucleus genes, it sacrifices the whole cell and retains only the nucleus, whereas the mother offers a complete cell surrounding the genetic nucleus.

We thus have an interesting and probably significant phenomenon. Among others, within the cell are organelles called mitochondria whose job is to utilize oxygen. Mitochondria have their own DNA, and they also have an independent, separate hereditary transmission. Since the sperm has eschewed the cell along with its organelles, then every descendant has nuclear DNA from the mother, nuclear DNA from the father, and mitochondrial DNA only from the mother. Every progeny is more mother than father, and many important traits, for instance, some of the supervision of sex hormones, are controlled by mitochondrial DNA and are therefore passed on to both offspring only by the mother. We now have two genders. One gender has the big gamete, which nourishes and also bequeaths mitochondria—and that is the mother. The second gender has a tiny, mitochondria-less gamete—and that is the father. From this point on, they are doomed to seek their mate in the 50% of the population, which are the opposite sex.

The differentiation process between the types of gametes deepened to the size in birds wherein the mother's gamete, the egg, is enormous, and the father's is invisible to the naked eye. The contrast in humans is also great. The mother's ovum is 50,000 times bigger than the father's seed. To this initial difference are added more and more attributes, structures, and behaviors, which constitute different "strategies" for each gender. The male produces about 100 million spermatozoa in one ejaculation, each one extremely small and hence cheap, so that there is no problem in manufacturing it. In stark contrast, the female works hard for a whole month to mature just one ovum, and in her entire lifetime she will produce only about 400.

A great distinction is also found in time investment. Let us look at the woman. What is the minimal time she must invest in every child? She gives up one month to mature the ovum, nine months of pregnancy, and if she suckles it for only two months, we have reached a year. The man's investment is 10 quite enjoyable minutes in transferring the sperm to the woman's womb, and even if we add the time it will take him to drive her to the maternity hospital, all in all his time investment is 30 minutes. So with mothers having to invest a year and fathers half an hour, we have a situation in which men can father a new baby every night, whereas women can produce only one a year. Does this make men superfluous? If a healthy man can inseminate a new child every night, even giving him a reduction for weekends and holidays, he can still produce 300 kids a year. The optimal sex ratio, then, should be 300 women to one man.

As we all know, there is no such population. In most species, offspring are born at a ratio of approximately 50:50 males to females. The answer was indicated by the eminent geneticist, Ronald Fisher. Males and females are born in similar numbers simply because natural selection acts on the interests of the individual not of the group. If there were a population of 300 females and one male, then a couple of parents who happened to have genes for producing sons would have been selected. Since sons would have hundreds of grandchildren and daughters only about three to four, evolutionary superiority would belong to the parents who could produce male offspring. This talent would have spread like fire. A few generations later, we would find too many boys, and then evolution would select parents who had genes for girls. Then, a few generations later, there would be too many girls. And so the pendulum swings, until it settles on an evolutionary stable strategy (ESS), which is about 50:50. It is stable simply because there is no evolutionary advantage in digressing from it. Did selection make do with individual parents only and not with whole groups? This is a fierce professional debate. Many think group selection is part of evolution. Others emphasize the selfish gene as the unit of selection. Still others stick to the individual organism. As was stated in the first chapter, at any level of particles' organization, a selection process takes place. Much smaller entities than genes compete for the stable form selection: atoms, molecules, and substances have to survive long enough in order to create genes, which survive long enough to create organisms, that create groups. At any layer of our world selection acts, and there are groups with different sex ratios. But still, in mammals Fisher's ESS is good enough.

As we well know, producing offspring is just the beginning. Now, mainly in the mammalian family, we must raise them, and that is a serious, time-consuming investment of effort, energy, money, anxiety, sleepless nights, tutoring, nurturing, and nutrient persuasion. Parents' resources for this type of parental investment are, for sure, limited, as we have learned from the sharp-witted American biologist, Robert Trivers. Over time, evolution has selected a parent who shrewdly distributed parental resources to as many children as possible.

Relegation of much of the work to the other is, no doubt, one way to parent many offspring.

We could imagine the following scenario: Two parents have a child. They know that it will not survive without parental investment, but each seeks to relegate more of it to the other. Evolutionary gain is in store for the one who manages to escape first, and dump the child and the work onto the other, while becoming free to continue reproducing. Who will escape first? This is a complex dilemma. When the mother asks herself: If I run away now, can I rely on him to stay with the child? The answer is, probably, "no." Why would he stay? What was his investment? What does he stand to lose if the child is lost now? So, she doesn't trust him. On the other hand, he can definitely rely on her. Why? Because she has already invested at least a year. Moreover, says Richard Dawkins, if she would want to start all over again, she would have to invest another year. So, she doesn't leave, and she continues to invest and increase her commitment and responsibility, more and more. Therefore, if anyone were to leave, in most cases it would probably be the man. For example, 1993 statistics on the Afro-American population in the United States reveal that 57% of all Afro-American children grow up in single-parent families, and a decisive majority of them with mothers. Of all children in the United States, 28% are raised in single-parent homes, almost exclusively by mothers.

The main danger threatening the mother in the game of the sexes is desertion. The male commitment to family is much weaker than the female's. What will the abandoned female do? Her best action is to find a substitute father. If she knows someone who is good, gentle, and kind, who will help her raise her children, instead of the rogue father who ran off—good. But the adoptive parent's kindness is not hereditary; an adoptive parent is an evolutionary dead end. From whom did the adopted child inherit its genes? From its scoundrel father, who said he was going out for a pack of cigarettes and never returned. The child is destined to be genetically similar to the deserting father, and not to the noble, adoptive one. In this state of affairs, when the female is looking for a substitute father, evolution will favor careful males, who successfully cope with the central danger threatening every man, the uncertainty as to who the father really is. Male parental investment is so minimal that it can hardly be detected in the offspring. With the mother, the question of whether the child is really hers never arises. With the father, there is always a question. Fathers will be selected by their ability to guarantee their fatherhood.

One common phenomenon that occurs in this context is the slaying of young infants. When a new male overpowers a group of females—in langures for instance—the first thing he does is systematically kill all the young, male or female descendants of another male. He clears for himself the parental potential of all the females around. Male chimpanzees may kill infants even if they are two to three years old, when the mother has migrated from one group to another, and therefore paternal uncertainty is high. In lions, the phenomenon is well known: a new ruler kills off all the young. Opportunistically enough, the females are in heat within two to three days. If their young had not been slain, it might have taken two to three years, and in chimpanzees five to six years. The stimulation of a new male and the infanticide bring on oestrus and assure the females of the essential presence of a male in the territory.

Killing infants is a terrible practice but not unknown among humans either. In the Book of Numbers, Chapter 31, we read the instructions Moses gave the soldiers of Israel, after their victory over the Midianites: "And Moses said unto them. . . . Now therefore kill every male among the little ones, and kill every woman that hath known man by lying with him, but all the women children, that have not known man by lying with him, keep alive for yourselves." This is a cruel sentence, and yet it occurs in apes, lions, and humans alike. A less cruel strategy is abortion. In rats, a new male may meet a pregnant female and generate a strong smell that causes her to abort. In humans, the doctor performs the abortion, which supplies a solution for box sexes. The female who was forsaken finds herself a new male, who ascertains his paternity. A period of delay is a less cruel, yet effective, method. If the pair defer before they decide, they will have a chance to examine each other. She will probably inspect his future loyalty, while he will probably check out paternity certainty. First you "date" and then you marry.

This practice can also be found in the Bible. In the Book of Deuteronomy, Chapter 21, we find instructions in case of war. "When thou goest forth to battle against thine enemies . . . and seest among the captives a woman of goodly form, and thou hast a desire unto her, and wouldest take her to thee to wife, then thy shalt bring her home to thy house . . . and shall remain in thy house . . . a full month, and after that thou mayest go in unto her, and be her husband, and she shall be thy wife." One month of caution is just right to make sure that the woman is not pregnant with another man's child.

From the moment of differentiation between the sexes, the two kinds of gametes, many additional traits, behaviors, and features were selected for each gender separately, according to its given opening characteristics, so that it would maximize children and grandchildren. Two different evolutionary roads were taken by each sex. Male and female are dissimilar because the strategies that promote the special interests of each are necessarily different. Thus, sexuality makes male and female dependent upon each other, yet at the same time turns them into competitors, and even combatants.

11

SEXUAL STRATEGIES

The previous chapter discussed the differences between the sexes in parental investment, and hence the dangers that face each sex. The female makes a big investment and is therefore threatened by desertion; the male makes a small investment and is therefore prone to paternal uncertainty. We can always know who the mother is, but we cannot be sure about the father's identity. As a result, each sex has evolved behavior strategies that try to cope with the dangers and to advance its own self-interests. There are many and varied such strategies. Richard Dawkins grouped them all into two representative strategies, which are, to a large extent, relevant also to humans.

Dawkins called the first strategy "domestic bliss strategy." The female, who is due to stake her best and carries out most of the parental investment, is in no hurry. She will not enter into a partnership with just anyone, and under any circumstance, she will inspect and investigate. She will mainly examine whoever can convince her that he will be devoted, that he will be of assistance. And as she waits, before giving her consent, she is actually expecting investment from him—that he prove his talents, that he seek out a territory and defend it, that he pay her dowry, buy her a diamond ring, solve the riddle of the Sphinx.

Among birds, the female sometimes regresses to infantile behavior. She sits there, pitifully, like a fledgling, and thus she stimulates the male to come and feed her. A male pigeon, courting a female, gives her parental care par excellence: he opens his beak and lets the virgin suckle his crop milk. Only after she drinks her fill will she allow him to copulate. In suckling his mate, the male contributes his own parental investment to egg production. In weavers, males painstakingly weave the nest all alone. When the job is done, the "lady" does a bit of quality inspection. She tosses the nest around with her beak, and if it falls apart, then he must construct it all over again. The essence of the "domestic bliss strategy" is in the female encouraging the male to greater parental investment. She involves him in her own high level of commitment and hence reduces the threat of desertion. When one has invested a lot, one is in no hurry to take off. This strategy will succeed only if all females take the same line and closely examine who they are dealing with. If, sometime along evolution, a female appears who does not delay, does not examine, and bestows herself quickly, she will be very successful because soon enough all the males will jump at the chance to invest as little as possible. In time, however, she will pay a high price, for she will get no support from any male. The pendulum will soon swing to the alternate conduct, and then, again, the careful female will thrive.

In today's modern Western society, most fathers are expected to invest a great deal, are committed to their families, and give their best. Yet, we often see the phenomenon of men who do not forgo the chance to do something cheap on the side. In fact, many men adopt a dual strategy. On the one hand, they conform to the "domestic bliss strategy"; they are committed, they invest, they are devoted, and on the other hand, they seek a furtive "quickie" in which the evolutionary rationale is: if you have an opportunity, use it, there is nothing to lose. Men, of course, risk less than women in a "quickie" strategy. Risk differences are apparently behind the statistics from all over the Western world, which indicate that about 55% of all married men are not sexually faithful to their mates, as opposed to about 25% of married women who are unfaithful. Since the main threat to the female is desertion, she hugely stresses the choice of a trustworthy male. She will shrewdly and meticulously investigate who can be trusted.

My mentor and friend Professor Daniel Freedman conducted a study at the University of Chicago in which female students were shown pictures of strange men. The pictures were altered three times. The same man appeared once clean-shaven, once with a mustache, and once with a beard. The students were asked: "How far would you trust which man?" A large sample of hundreds of women revealed that the one perceived as most reliable was the clean-shaven one, and the least reliable—the man with the mustache. Since it was the same man in all three cases, the experiment exposed a sort of caution mechanism, which was selected in women in order to help them be wary of the one who was liable to desert them.

It is interesting to note that shaving the facial hair, which is actually cutting off a significant male crownlet, is seen by women as a sign of better parenthood. When a man is more like a woman, who has no beard, he might act more like her, stay home, and care for the kids. It seems that the same goes for head-hair. Bald men are perceived as more trustworthy, more parental, and more affectionate. Since women are so painstaking in their search for the one who will be faithful, evolution selects the man who can convince them how faithful he is; that is to say, it selects the deceiver. Evolution will give a bonus to the charlatan, who manages to convince her that he will "be yours forever," thus securing her heart and womb, and then will abandon and go on his way to reproduce many children. But evolution will not like the woman who is easily fooled. Therefore, as measures against the con man, evolution selects an even more suspicious woman. And when women become more distrustful, evolution will select better liars in men, and then women will be even more distrustful, and men—even better liars.

This process of improvement ultimately produces the consummate liar: the person who totally believes his own lies. He is indeed convinced that he loves her in a way never known before on earth, that he will stay with her forever, that there is no other woman like her, never will be, and never has been. Self-deception is an important psychological mechanism. We find it, for instance, in psychological "defense mechanisms"—those tricks that relieve distress and are effective only if the person is not aware that he is cheating himself. They can usually be identified by external secondary signs. The external signs that point to a case of self-deception in lovers, who vow "eternity," is their delirious, manic, dazzled, and blinded excitement. Romance is endowed with shortsightedness, and that is in its best interest. The word "romance" brings to mind an image of a white veil fluttering in the wind. A veil covers bitter facts that might ruin the illusion of perfect love. Each of us, for sure, knows what goes on around us. We can all see our family, and that of neighbors, friends, and relatives, and realize that love is not eternal. It dies at some stage, and yet when two people are in love they promise each other over and over again that their love, and only theirs, is forever. The mutual perfection of fraud and suspicion also endures after marriage. It does not occur only during the choice of a mate but continues in the long run. After children are born and the two carry on as a couple, they find a lot of deception and a great deal of suspicion in the question of fidelity versus infidelity.

Dawkins called the other major sexual strategy the "he-man strategy." Both sexes employ this strategy in order to avoid their respective pitfalls—fear of desertion in women and paternal uncertainty in men. They do it by carrying the differences between them to the extreme. From the start, the female takes into account that the male will not participate in the parental efforts, and she allows herself to use one criterion only—to choose the most qualitative sperm, for without it she can do nothing. She makes do with seed but wants it from the he-man, the best. He does not bother to examine paternity because he does not invest anything beyond cheap semen.

An example of this strategy can be found in the Israeli ibex of the Judean Desert. They spend their lives in separate groups at different locations. Females roam the Valley of King David, and males climb the Pillars of King Solomon. They meet only in autumn during the oestrus period, when they descend to the grassy shores of the Dead Sea. Using their horns, the males compete in the choice of the he-man; the females sit around and watch from the sidelines. "Let the young men, I pray you, arise and play before us." After three or four days of exhausting battles, the he-man is chosen and is awarded most of the mating. The offspring is raised by the mother alone.

In most species, males are not horned. How, then, is the he-man chosen? For lack of genetic testing, females rely on their eyes and whatever sensory perception they can use. That is why they mostly all agree about who the he-man is, who will be awarded the most couplings. This forces males into fierce competition, with each wanting to be THE one. They fight for the right. This is probably the initial and leading reason for the evolution of the strong status struggles that agitate every society to this day. Status hierarchy is a considerable factor in female choice. A male who succeeds in climbing to the top of the status hierarchy is granted the most mating. Females look and examine the males' status. They do the right thing when they choose a high-status male to father their children, because in this way they transmit the promising genes of a prosperous male, and if their children are equally successful, they will gain many grandchildren.

In one group of seals, it was found that 4% of the males, those at the top of the status hierarchy, fathered 85% of the next generation. At times, the status struggle in seals is so powerful, and the effort to serve most of the females after the victory is so fierce, that at the end of the season many of these males die. But they have left something behind as their legacy, and evolution indeed loves those who battle for status. In humans, a similar phenomenon flourishes in what sociologists call "marrying up." Women aim to find a husband with high status, or at least higher than their own.

The Mormons might be a modern example. Linda Mealey has probed the evolutionary advantages of the status hierarchy. Mormon men used to marry a number of wives, as many as each one's wealth would allow (until polygamy was banned in the state of Utah in 1892). There were, therefore, big differences in the number of children each Mormon had. A clear status hierarchy differentiated Mormon men, mainly in church rank, which was correlated with financial power. Data compiled about the Mormons in the nineteenth century indicate that the higher a man's status, the more wives he had and, of course, the more children.

What else do females look for in the he-man male? Survival ability is a cardinal overall indicator of success in the rough savanna. How does one check someone's ability to survive? Age is one test. If he is older, he has survived many trials, and indeed women tend to seek an older man, at least older than themselves. The ability to provide is another good criterion. Who is a good provider? A good hunter. Who is a good hunter? The one with the muscles, the tall, athletic, handsome one. At a later period, intelligence became a significant factor. That might be the reason, when they start dating, that he quotes Einstein and discusses postmodernism. His intelligence is being examined through the brilliant, enlightened, erudite discourse during courting foreplay.

All the excellent genes we mentioned are invisible and are represented by external signs. Natural selection fosters pronounced extraneous symbols, sometimes to the point of nothing more than an empty facade. A tiresome example is the peacock's tail, which is so very magnificent that it is hard to grasp how the peacock paved his way in the jungle. The peacock's tail is such a burden that no one studying evolution would dare to avoid elucidating this paradox. The evolution of this tail was not for its practical advantages, but for its significant symbolism. It is possible that all the splendor started with one feather decorated with an eye, which was meant to declare: "I am a peacock, not a turkey." Then evolution liked the one that had, by chance, two eyes on its tail, because it was an outstanding peacock. And then three eyes, which said: am the most peacock of all." And so the tail developed, until it became a serious nuisance but a very distinctive sign.

Let us, now, consider the she-peacock. If she is wise, she will say: "I am not impressed by all this showing off. I don't care about the tail. I want him kind and modest." She might, then, choose a gray male. For her own private life, this is probably a good choice, but she is courting trouble for her offspring because they will be born without the magnificent tail. Hence, they will not be chosen by the females of the next generation, who are just ordinary hens and behave according to the norm. There is an important lesson here for human life as well: Be like everyone else. Don't put on wise airs. Don't deviate. Go with the mainstream; otherwise, you'll be punished.

Adherence to an external sign, which is just a front, cannot go on ad infinitum. It will stop when the price becomes too high. An outstanding example of this is the Irish elk, which has been extinct for some 10,000 years.

Its impressive horn span reached 4 meters. It was very sexy, for sure, but difficult to live with and the deer could not survive.

The first "domestic bliss strategy" is dominant in humans. The male invests a lot more than sperm. His commitment is strong, and he too must be careful in his choice of mate. What does the male examine? Since he knows that the woman is destined to do most of the parental work, he will take this into account. He looks for the fertile and the motherly. Again, outward appearance represents these characteristics, which cannot be noticed in any other way. Fertility is expressed in a young, healthy physique, which is perceived as proportional, soft, and a good figure. This is why a woman's physical attractiveness has such a powerful influence on the man while he selects.

A woman's maternal capabilities are measured by her wide pelvis and her breasts, the human parallel of the peacock's tail. A wide pelvis is the mother's adaptation to the new, wise, overgrown head of her child. At the beginning of humanity, when the birth of the large head was a critical motherly trial, and many mothers died while delivering, evolution selected a man who would be attracted to wide hips. How are wide hips judged? With the eyes. And how do we judge with the eyes? By assessing the waist-to-hip ratio. The smaller the ratio, the more desirable she is. It was reported by Devendra Singh that women whose waist-hip ratio is less than 0.8 have higher levels of feminine hormones, like estrogens. That is to say, female hormones, mainly during the fertile years, are responsible not only for fecundity, but also for the external maternal appearance, which attracts men. At menopause, estrogen levels decline and as a result, the waist to hip ratio increases. Women who want to seem attractive accentuate their wide hips by keeping their stomachs flat. This could very well be the reason for the success of an old and stable fashion industry, women's belts.

Breasts represent female aptitude to suckle, but there is no correlation whatsoever between breast size and ability to breast-feed. Female chimpanzees make excellent mothers, who suckle their young for four to six years, yet they are equipped with only nipples and milk glands, no breasts. Breasts are a promotional gimmick, an enlarged symbol. They are a splendid ruse that manages to fool men and attract them, but their entire job is to impress. As was the case with the she-peacock, who was obliged to select the he-man's extravagant tail, so is the case for women, who must grow, carry, and show their wonderful breasts, and so is the case of men who cannot deny its attractivity. A woman born without breasts could still be a perfect mother, but she would be stuck at an earlier stage: no man would want her as a wife. Indeed, women try to impress men exactly with what men consider important. They try to be young and pretty, maintain a shapely figure, and look healthy and maternal, with full breasts and rounded buttocks.

When we examine which topics both sexes falsify, while groping toward potential bonding, we find that men cheat about their future trustworthiness, commitment, and economic capabilities. On the other hand, women deceive men about their appearance. They do not tell their age, nor do they divulge their dependence on intensive cosmetic treatments, hair dyes, or heavy dieting. Evolution, which stresses worthwhile signals in mates, also invites deceit about these very signs.

oestrus. Over 90% of mammalian females have oestrus and so are sexually active for only a few days. But human females, as we know, are sexually active all year long. The second special characteristic is the increasing dissociation of sex and reproduction. A negligible amount of human sexual activity is devoted to pure reproduction. On the contrary, most human sexual activity is performed with care and attention to contraception. The third important characteristic is the long-term relationship, the lifetime contract, which we call marriage.

Let us do the following exercise in order to explain these evolutionary adaptations of the human species. About 8 million years ago, humans and chimpanzees had a common ancestor. After the east-west split, chimps remained in the tropical forest, which was our forefathers' "correct" natural environment; they have therefore altered very little in the ensuing 8 million years. Humans lost the forest, were thrown naked onto the savanna, and made the long journey to the humane marriages that characterize our society today. We could view present-day chimpanzees as a kind of starting point from which we departed 8 million years ago, and we could see ourselves as the finish line, and try to bridge the two ends of the continuum by means of a few assumptions.

What are chimpanzees like? In his finely documented book *The Evolution of Human Sexuality*, the American anthropologist Donald Symons describes the sexual behavior of chimpanzees. Their social structure is one of a stable group in which a number of males cooperate in protection of the territory. This might be the very beginning of the famous and glorious human male frater-nity-in-arms. By guarding the territory, they also maintain the sexual exclusiv-ity of their females, so that no strange male can invade their boundary and fertilize an innocent wanderer. Females roam the territory in small, intimate groups of two or three and their offspring. The female chimps begin to menstruate at the age of 11–12 and become fertile around the age of 13–14. Just as in humans, two to three years pass between the onset of menstruation and fertility. Oestrus can appear at any time during the year at no set season. For a number of days the female "consents," and the rest of the year she refuses sex. She must, of course, advertise the fact that she is willing, and she does indeed advertise on two channels. The first channel is scent. She spreads scent particles, pheromones, all around, and males gather from the ends of the earth. The other channel, which is evolutionarily much more recent, is visual. The female demonstrates her availability by means of inflated nipples and buttocks.

After the female has been impregnated and given birth, she breastfeeds the infant for five to six years. During this period she is not in heat. The contraceptive is the hormone prolactin, which first and foremost is responsible for milk production, but as we have noted, has other roles, including the prevention of ovulation. As long as the nipple is stimulated by suckling, the oestrus. Over 90% of mammalian females have oestrus and so are sexually active for only a few days. But human females, as we know, are sexually active all year long. The second special characteristic is the increasing dissociation of sex and reproduction. A negligible amount of human sexual activity is devoted to pure reproduction. On the contrary, most human sexual activity is performed with care and attention to contraception. The third important characteristic is the long-term relationship, the lifetime contract, which we call marriage.

Let us do the following exercise in order to explain these evolutionary adaptations of the human species. About 8 million years ago, humans and chimpanzees had a common ancestor. After the east-west split, chimps remained in the tropical forest, which was our forefathers' "correct" natural environment; they have therefore altered very little in the ensuing 8 million years. Humans lost the forest, were thrown naked onto the savanna, and made the long journey to the humane marriages that characterize our society today. We could view present-day chimpanzees as a kind of starting point from which we departed 8 million years ago, and we could see ourselves as the finish line, and try to bridge the two ends of the continuum by means of a few assumptions.

What are chimpanzees like? In his finely documented book *The Evolution of Human Sexuality*, the American anthropologist Donald Symons describes the sexual behavior of chimpanzees. Their social structure is one of a stable group in which a number of males cooperate in protection of the territory. This might be the very beginning of the famous and glorious human male frater-nity-in-arms. By guarding the territory, they also maintain the sexual exclusiv-ity of their females, so that no strange male can invade their boundary and fertilize an innocent wanderer. Females roam the territory in small, intimate groups of two or three and their offspring. The female chimps begin to menstruate at the age of 11–12 and become fertile around the age of 13–14. Just as in humans, two to three years pass between the onset of menstruation and fertility. Oestrus can appear at any time during the year at no set season. For a number of days the female "consents," and the rest of the year she refuses sex. She must, of course, advertise the fact that she is willing, and she does indeed advertise on two channels. The first channel is scent. She spreads scent particles, pheromones, all around, and males gather from the ends of the earth. The other channel, which is evolutionarily much more recent, is visual. The female demonstrates her availability by means of inflated nipples and buttocks.

After the female has been impregnated and given birth, she breastfeeds the infant for five to six years. During this period she is not in heat. The contraceptive is the hormone prolactin, which first and foremost is responsible for milk production, but as we have noted, has other roles, including the prevention of ovulation. As long as the nipple is stimulated by suckling, the pituitary gland in the brain continues to produce more prolactin, and there will be no additional pregnancy. As to male fertility, like humans, chimpanzees have constant, continuous sexual alertness. Semen appears at the age of 9–10, but first intercourse does not occur before the age of 11–12, an age at which, status-wise, they have control over most of the females but not yet over the males. Status struggles against other males, which determine sexual rights, begin to multiply later on, and only around the age of 13–15 does the young male find himself somewhere along the status hierarchy and is awarded copulation accordingly.

A very interesting sexual behavior in chimpanzees is "promiscuous" mating. A female chimpanzee in heat will stand "on a high hill under a spreading tree," with an orderly, polite line of males waiting their turn. They jump her one after the other with no quarrels and no animosity. At face value, this phenomenon was supposed to send many evolutionary theories crashing, mainly that males should battle for the right and that females should choose the triumphant, dominant, most handsome male. How could all these be explained by free sex for whoever is hungry? Indeed, this indifferent sex baffled researchers, but after careful examination, it was found that the rulers copulated the most. Moreover, their encounter with the female is at a time when she is most likely to conceive. That is to say, their chance to father offspring is much higher than that of a marginal male, who usually gets fewer opportunities during the remote days of oestrus.

A contrasting phenomenon can also be found in chimpanzees—exclusive consortship. A couple may retire to the far end of the territory and spend a long period of time on their own under the bushes. Two things happen during this time: intercourse, of course, and—a splendid surprise—the male pampering of the females. He grooms her fur a lot, picks lice attentively, and brings her goodies to eat. Indeed, she is amply awarded for her favors. This consortship is probably a female initiative, in which she apparently gains more than she loses. Her loss is in coupling with a subordinate rather than a dominant male. The dominant male would not have joined her, because he has many females, and he does not have to make do with one. In return for waiving status, she gains the coddling, which is a form of parental investment. In some cases, however, the male forces the female to follow him to remote areas by violently attacking her, reminding us that, quite often, sexuality does go with aggression.

A very important chimpanzee characteristic is food sharing. Chimpanzees are mostly vegetarians, but still about 6 to 10% of their food-basket is meat. Meat, mainly small animals, are hunted by the adult males, who eat them themselves and sometimes bring a bit home. And who do they give it to? The female in heat and her offspring. She gives, and so she takes. This portrayal of the chimpanzee meat-economy may perhaps explain an ingenious female innovation: oestrus cancellation. A female who, by chance, is in heat for a longer period (there is a distribution around the average in every phenomenon) obtains a larger portion of meat. When the exile from forest to savanna caused meat to become a more important component of the food-basket, natural selection strongly preferred females whose oestrus was longer and longer, and they transmitted this trait to their daughters. Thus, from generation to generation, females whose oestrus extended over more days were selected, until we have modern females whose oestrus continues all year round.

An early example of oestrus exploitation for purposes other than procreation was discovered by the American biologist Sarah Hrdy. This sharp-eyed, sharp-minded scientist noticed that females act cunningly with greedy males of the langur monkeys. When a new male takes over a group of females, he system-atically kills all the young and will continue killing any infant that will be born in the future months. A female who is already pregnant by the previous male pretends to be in heat and encourages the new male to jump her, and later on proudly father the infant to be born. A devoted mother, she pulls the wool over his eyes and thus saves her unborn child. This pretense can perhaps also be a way to gain more food. The female must publicize the fact that she is in heat, so that the males are aware of it and give her due attention and honor. Human women extend not only oestrus over the entire year, but also the announcement of it. If chimpanzees advertise oestrus by means of inflated nipples and buttocks, then women carry constant advertisements in the form of breasts and buttocks, which are constantly enlarged. The extension of oestrus and the building of the ad itself in a woman's body structure make human female sexuality a way to trade in foodstuffs.

To this day, among some tribes in South America, we can witness the following scene. A lazy husband, spending many long siesta hours in his hammock, fails to supply the family's meat. His wife, after warning him again and again, dresses up, puts on her finest trinkets, swings her hips, and goes out to seduce other men. She threatens him with the removal of her sexuality if he denies her livelihood. She owes her conjugal rights to the man who supplies her food. Now her man must make a swift decision—either get up and provide for her, or lose his rights over her sexuality, which means fatherhood, and remain childless, which is an evolutionary dead end. The new human contract, marriage, assures human men a lot of sex, much more than other eager males in nature get. Man is overjoyed by his woman's new, abundant sexuality, but because of the threat of uncertainty, he must keep it all for himself. Since there are no oestrus days, the human male is in a unique situation. He does not know when the female is fertile, and he must therefore guard her sexuality, so that he does not end up raising someone else's children. Consequently, he must return home every night. And so he does, equipped with meat, and he secures paternal certainty by having total ownership of her sexuality. Hence, men and women enter into an economic-sexual agreement in which each side gives and takes.

In Israel, every man who gets married signs a *ketubah*, a marriage certificate, in which he vows to provide his wife's maintenance. This is his part of the contract. The Rabbinical court, which is the only way to get in and out of marriage, will enable him to divorce her if she is not exclusive in her sexuality, because that is her part of the contract. If chimpanzees' sexuality was the starting point and humans' sexuality today is the end, then the three unique characteristics of our sexuality perhaps appeared in this order: first *extinction, or extension, of oestrus*. The woman was found to be in heat for longer and longer periods of time, obtained more meat, and so continued oestrus all year round. In return for the meat and to assure sexual exclusivity, continuous sexuality between regular partners was selected. Hence, *the close connection between sex and reproduction ended*. Reproductive sex was replaced by sexuality aimed at maintaining the couple's relationship. Sexuality has now become a sort of glue by which men and women sustain their constant, intimate relationship. This is the platform for the third characteristic—the *long-term relationship*—which is a sexual-economic contract for raising children. Today we call it family.

The family is perhaps the most important and most powerful human phenomenon, its power stemming from the fact that it solves the supreme interests of either side. The family is good for the woman, who is the main parental investor and hence the party who is most likely to be deserted; thus, she is eager for parental partnership with the man and his long-term faithfulness. That is exactly what the family affords her. The family contract is also beneficial to the man because when he invests in his children (and raising young on the savanna is nearly impossible without him), he wants to be sure that they are indeed his children. Only the woman's long-term fidelity will give him relatively high certainty on this issue. The treat, which unites these interests, is sexuality. The sexual act, which was selected a long time ago as a means to reproduce and was designed as a pleasure in order to reward a truly correct evolutionary deed, has been converted to grant an additional advantage—to reward the partners in the parental effort. The children will reach maturity only through the dual effort of both parents, and in them the craving for two parents, mother and father, was selected. The self-interests of all parties meet in the family, and in that it is a central product of human sexuality.

Human sexuality is also singular in the external sexual accessories of our bodies, which are very pronounced. Man's penis is big and prominent in comparison to that of apes, and so are woman's breasts and buttocks. These

13

EVOLUTION OF THE FAMILY

It is hard to overrate the importance of the family in human evolution. To a great extent, the family epitomizes the uniqueness of humanity. In human evolution, as in the private lives of each and every one of us, the family is where our shape is formed; the family is yearning; the family is fate. In reconstructing the evolution of human preeminence step by step, we seek the first step, the incentive that separated us from the chimpanzees.

Anthropology has probed two candidates for this role: our big head, which holds a brain three times the size of a chimpanzee's, and bipedality, which is so uniquely human. We esteem the human mind highly; anthropologists tend to regard our bigger brain as the first lever, from a timetable point of view. But the correct answer is the opposite one, and it was demonstrated by Lucy, a lady who lived on the Ethiopian prairie 3 to 4 million years ago. She stood upright on two feet, whereas she had a chimpanzee's 450 cubic centimeter brain. Following the discovery of Lucy's skeleton by the American anthropologist Donald Johanson, and others of her species, including skull 444 which was found by the Israeli Yoel Rak, in which the opening of the spinal chord in the base of the skull definitely points to uprightness, the argument was closed. Today there is general consent that the first evolutionary cornerstone was uprightness, which as suggested by the American Owen Lovejoy, is closely related to family evolution.

If we were to take a number of monkeys and line them up on an evolutionary continuum from ancient to later and to ape and to humans, we would have the following: lemur, macaque, gibbon, chimpanzee, human. We observe progressive transformation from lemur to human on a number of demographic parameters—for instance, a lengthier pregnancy term, a longer and longer childhood, a more prolonged life expectancy. The chimpanzee's life expectancy is 40 years, and the human's is 70. The proportions between these components are fixed. If human life expectancy is the longest, then our pregnancies and childhood are also the most prolonged. Those who manage to achieve greater life expectancy and lengthier childhood must conceive an answer to the dangers threatening humans during their most vulnerable period. In order to attain higher life expectancy, the weakest part of the chain—infants—must be protected. Jane Goodall, the distinguished British researcher, indicates that chimpanzees maintain a very intense mother–infant bond for five to six years and that this intensity prevents an additional pregnancy. The two main causes of infant mortality in chimpanzees, she states, are malfunction of the mother–infant attachment and falls. The infant falls from the mother, mainly while she is running or climbing a tree. If the human ape managed to increase its life expectancy, we would suppose that it had succeeded in adapting a good solution to the maintenance of mother–child contact with a minimal number of deaths.

Due to the sensitivity of the mother–infant contact, some monkeys, as well as other animals, tend to divide feeding areas between males and females. For example, the females take to the tree tops with the young, and the males have their meals halfway down the tree. This allotment is meant to facilitate mother–infant mobility. The tree tops are richer in food and offer better protection from predators. When humans stepped down off from the trees and took to wandering the savanna, the division between males and females became centrifugal rather than vertical. Males roam larger distances, whereas females and young ones are stationary. Under the rough conditions of the arid land, this concession of the male is evolutionarily "correct," only if it furthers the well-being of his own mate and offspring. When chimpanzee males find a rich food source, they call food-cries and invite the entire group to a good meal. This is a kind of group mutual assistance, which could develop in the abundance of a tropical paradise, where a lush environment permits its inhabitants to be generous. But in humans, when food became hard to come by and father's participation in feeding the young became essential (and hence male's certainty that he was indeed feeding his own children became more important), he no longer made public announcements when he happened upon food. Instead, he gathered it and carried it in his hands back to share with his offspring and mate.

Unlike other feeding parents in nature, such as birds and predators, humans are not equipped with conveyance accessories, such as a beak or jaws, that can carry booty home. Hands are therefore the alternative. Hands, which are freed when the body is upright, are the means by which to bring food home. Human parents may well have risen to bipedality for the sake of their fragile kids in the cruel savanna. The stationary mother gathers food in her close surroundings and bears it home, whereas the mobile father bears his booty. The human father began participating in the child-rearing tasks. The result was significant enhancement of parental success—more survival of children.

The female chimpanzee is a wonderful mother. The male chimpanzee is a warrior, a bully who protects his territory, but is not a good father. He does not take care of his offspring; in fact, he can hardly tell them apart from other young ones in the group. It sometimes happens that a male kidnaps and preys upon an infant which may be his own progeny. When the human man turned from simply a male into a father and joined the universal loving mother–infant duo as a third party, he enabled proliferation of the family, and that family is the fertile cradle of human preeminence. Two parents represent a strong survival force, lessening infant mortality and allowing for decreased gaps between births. Whereas chimpanzees have a new baby within six years, the interval in humans is down to four. Some families raise a number of siblings simultaneously. A family in which Mom, Dad, and a number of kids spend every evening together is a major momentum for the development of social relations via sophisticated communication.

The most distinctive human features, the large brain and high intelligence, may be the result of evolving social talents rather than of expanding technological expertise. Humans experience a rich and intense sociability in the group, mainly within the family. In ancient times, family members gathered round the fire in the evening, shared food, and nurtured kinship and empathy. Each told of the day's achievements and disappointments, shared a feeling of togetherness, and mourned their dead. Fire works magic on our souls. Bonfires are especially pleasurable occasions, despite our era of electricity and electronics. When we mourn someone, we light memorial candles, the perpetual fire of family from time immemorial.

Playing is also a cardinal feature of family life. Mammals brought play into the world as part of the intense mother–infant contact. The limbic area of the brain supervises our playing. In humans play has reached a high degree of importance, serving two major objectives: it prepares the child for adulthood, and it inspires a relaxed and conciliatory atmosphere within the family. In play, real-life situations are practiced in hotbed conditions, with no fatal outcome, and with the opportunity to try over and over again. Many mammals play with their parents, who thus impart a cultural heritage. In this sense, play is the basis for education. Within the human family, it also helps the long childhood time to be experienced in a pleasant way and nurtures mutual love between family members.

The human family has taken various forms in different eras and cultures; yet the distinct tendency has been toward the nuclear monogamous family. In our chimpanzee brothers, monogamy is but a hint; their dominant social unit is the group. Humans put greater and greater emphasis on the nuclear family, consisting of two parents who promise each other eternal exclusivity. Monogamy, though not perfect, is a strong evolutionary tendency in humans. Most of today's human societies declared policy is monogamy, and people in the main view it positively. With regard to polygamy, many quote ethnographic statistics indicating that the majority of human cultures are polygamous rather than monogamous. But from the evolutionary standpoint, the significant question is this: How strong is the tendency toward fatherly participation in raising and supporting children? In polygamous societies, no less than in monogamous ones, a forcible emphasis is placed on paternal commitment. It is definitely a universal characteristic of the human species, which clearly separates us from the chimpanzees.

A monogamous sexual bond and paternal participation in children's rearing are dramatic adaptations from the ways of the chimpanzee. How was this adaptation implemented and by whom? To be sure, hormones are among the important mechanisms that supervise monogamous behavior (and any other behavior). In voles, mouselike rodents, we find both a monogamous and a polygamous population. The monogamous kind maintains a long-term relationship with one mate, and both parents share in raising the young. In the polygamous strain, the male copulates with a number of females, each in a different territory, and does not participate in infant nurturing.

A comparison of various sex and maternal hormone levels in monogamous versus polygamous voles reveals some interesting differences. A change in the dosage and timing of progesterone, for instance, permits endless copulation for the monogamous pair—as long as 30 to 40 straight hours. Their sexuality, just like ours, becomes a means whereby a couple bonds. Since they have sex for so long, and the female's vagina arousal stimulates the brain, it encourages the production of yet another maternal hormone called oxytocin. Like prolactin, oxytocin has a role in both milk production and initiation of close physical contact between mother and infant. Since the levels of oxytocin in monogamous voles are very high as a result of prolonged sexual activity, they continue to touch each other, groom, stroke, and enjoy warm physical non-sexual contact. Oxytocin can be injected into a vole's brain in order to obtain grooming social behavior. Alternatively, it could be blocked to cancel this social behavior. Here is a wonderful opportunity to see how warm emotional contact between adults draws its materials, such as hormones, from the repertoire of motherhood.

Another significant sex hormone is testosterone which induces masculine behavior in all males, including humans. Less testosterone means less masculinity. Stress on a male fetus during pregnancy could increase levels of stress hormones, such as cortisol. Cortisol, in its turn, tends to decrease testosterone levels so that as a result of a difficult pregnancy we will have a feminine, less masculine male. In a comparison of monogamous and polygamous voles, Carter and Getz, found in 1993, that the monogamous produce abundant quantities of stress hormones without being under stress. Why would that be? The answer is probably that stress hormones reduce testosterone levels and thus enable males to be more feminine, that is, more motherly. The same mechanism which in a polygamous male produces deficiency of masculinity, deliberately creates femininity in the monogamous male, so that the vole can be more maternal. The Emperor penguins of Antarctica are highly aggressive during the mating, nesting, and brooding period. Accordingly, their testosterone levels are very high. Sharp decreases in testosterone, as chicks break their eggs, turn both father and mother into gentle, soft parents.

In various rodents, and even in one type of monkey, the marmosets, where fathers are actively involved in child rearing, dramatic increases of the hormone prolactin were measured in male blood. Prolactin is a mothering hormone, but when the father is part of child-rearing or is next to his pregnant mate and smells the pheromones that proclaim the approaching birth, he becomes more maternal, more feminine. Hormones turn the tough male into a soft parent. If not for the hormonal change, the father might have devoured his offspring. Is it so in humans? Initial data suggest evidence of hormonal changes in men when their wives are pregnant. Some 25% seek doctors' help and complain of stomach aches, swelling, headaches, nausea, vomiting, and anorexia—all symptoms of hormonal change. I do not know of any studies that measure such hormonal changes, but future studies may find that the human father undergoes hormonal changes when he lives beside his pregnant wife and then beside his young children. The changes might be the result of increased prolactin and oxytocin, or decreased testosterone, or both and more.

Hormones play an important role in yet another central aspect of human family development—the division of labor between the sexes and the differentiation of talents and inclinations. Inasmuch as sex-role differences grew and deepened, natural selection ultimately made males better hunters and better warriors, and women better mothers and food gatherers. Sex hormones, mainly through influence on the fetus's brain, foster these talents. Testosterone, for example, and other androgens prepare the man to have a strong muscular body. A male fetus is already more robust than a female fetus, just as his brain is more masculine than that of a female fetus. Male higher aggression is a product of testosterone influence on the brain. Superior spatial perception and better navigation skills are testosterone dependent. The drive for leadership and status are fueled by testosterone. Estrogens, on the other hand, prepare the motherly body by producing wide hips and the attentive, responsive, tender female brain, and women's superior verbal skills. The faculty of speech is perhaps the basis for the dominance of the left verbal hemisphere over the right hemisphere, which in turn reinforces right-handedness. Doreen Kimura, the Canadian brain researcher, suggests that the very brain areas that perfected the praxis of females' dexterous hand are the ones that command speech flow.

The unique evolution of the human family reflected a zigzag move. It first honed the differences between the sexes—he a hunter, she a mother—and then brought them together as devoted parents. No doubt with the benediction of evolution, the father began to participate more and more in caring for the children, deepening his family involvement, and concern. Just like voles, the human male went through a process of feminization, becoming more caring, understanding, emotional, and empathic. That is, men became more like women.

This huge evolutionary process can be detected in the development of one child. In a study, I asked four groups of children, aged 5, 10, 15, and 20 (ages chosen to approximate a followup), which ideal traits they wished they had (Lampert forthcoming). At the age of five, it is very important for boys to be strong and brave which I considered the militancy factor. Five-year-old girls want to be a good mother and good-hearted which I considered the nurturing factor. In other words, at the age of 5 we find a division similar to that found in chimpanzees. He is a wrestler, and she is a mother. But over the next 15 years, boys gradually change their minds. If we ask the same questions, we receive quite different answers. The closer they get to age 20, the emphasis changes. They renounce militancy, and they acknowledge nurturing. Now they want to be good fathers, and good-hearted. Girls do not significantly change from 5 to 20. Since I gave my subjects a list of ideal traits to prefer whatever they wished, it is interesting to note that boys increased their nurturance at the expense of militancy. The two factors were significantly negatively correlated $r = 0.76$; $p < 0.01$. The single child thus recapitulates, in its own personal development, human evolution in its entirety. Instead of a militant male, he becomes a tender and loving father (see Figures 6, 7).

Figure 6
Development of Sex Differences in Militancy (*n*=80)

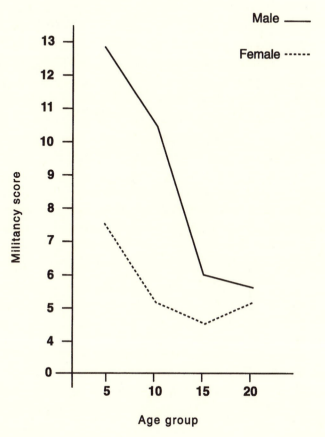

The feminization process of the human species does not sweep away all fields. There are areas in which the opposite is true. Women work outside the home and strive for worldly achievements and success, becoming prime ministers, engineers, pilots, lawyers, and so on. Within the family, however, the caring motherhood of chimpanzees has become a joint endeavor in humans, and joint parenthood is a highly important part of the human family.

All over the world, the wedding is regarded as the happy end, the ultimate solution to human happiness. This universal assumption is even more salient since plenty of evidence has accumulated that human happiness is to a great extent a congenital blessing. As Myers and Diener reported, some are simply born with a greater ability to be happy than others. This innate capability supersedes many other factors that used to be seen as conditions for happiness, notably, a pleasant childhood, a firm socioeconomic position, achievements,

Figure 7
Development of Sex Differences in Nurturing (*n*=80)

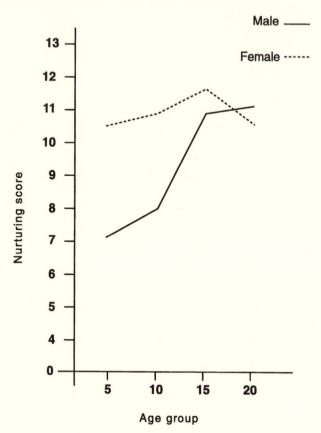

income, and even age. Whoever is born to happiness will feel it under almost all circumstances. Genetic happiness might be dented by harsh conditions, but on a daily basis, in a reasonable environment, it determines the degree of our happiness.

And yet, it has been systematically found that the degree of happiness is divided between two groups: singles who never married are less happy, and married people are happier. Moreover, those who are divorced are the unhappiest group of all. Of married people, 39% define themselves as "very happy," and of the never married, 24% are "very happy"; the figure drops to 12% in divorced people (see Figure 8). Life in a family setting seems to be the "correct situation" for "happiness genes," each according to their inborn ability. Lack of family is "incorrect" in the eyes of human evolution, and even those who are born to happiness will find it difficult without the cradle of securely belonging.

Figure 8
Marital Status and Happiness

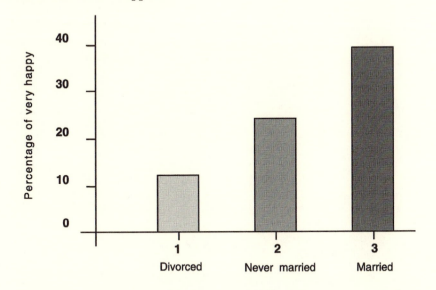

The power of marriage to cheer us up is certainly not so much due to formalities, as it is due to the proximity, touch, warmth, support, fondling and care that usually accompany marriage.

14

MATE SELECTION

A "family" in the sense of two parents devotedly raising common offspring over a long period is not unique to humans. It can be observed in many birds, voles, some monkeys, and more. But the intensity of feeling that occurs with family life reaches its peak in humans. Of all the many stormy feelings, the most prominent are those that are involved in the first steps of the family process: falling in love, selecting the partner with whom we will embark on the long journey of raising a family. Falling in love is, in many cases, an inexplicable experience. Who can speak rationally of its sensuous, dazzling, sweeping, overflowing nature? And yet, let us try to understand it in the spirit of this book, as an evolutionary product selected for its contribution to reproduction.

Falling in love is a dramatic component of mate selection. When we seek a mate, we look around, opening our eyes up wide. As opposed to other creatures, who open their nostrils to sniff, we open our eyes to gaze. And our eyes are drawn, as if by magic, to beauty. We strongly respond to beauty.

Moral edicts teach us to ignore beauty and instead to defend different values: "Look not on the jar, but on its contents." That is morality's way, to insist on the very issues that our hearts most hanker for; it stands in the breach of our sweeping impulses. Indeed, beauty catches our hearts, dazzles our eyes, and overrides our judgment, so that in lieu of it we tend to ignore the importance of wisdom, diligence, kindness, and other merits.

As a sworn-in Darwinist, I believe that if beauty has the power to awaken such yearning in us, then evolution selected and perfected this sensitivity as one of our many traits, which were all selected for their contribution to the ability to produce offspring. Why is sensitivity to beauty so important? Why has evolution toiled to wire into our brain and nervous system and the hormonal secretions in our blood mechanisms that respond with excitement and desire to "beautiful" and recoil from "ugly"?

Plato suggests what would later be seen as an exceedingly Darwinistic solution to this question. In his book *The Banquet*, clever Diotima teaches Socrates an important evolutionary lesson. She says:

> humans sow their seed . . . and when they come to a certain age, our nature yearns to breed, but with the ugly he cannot and with the beautiful he can. Since the coming together of man and woman—is procreation . . . and in the unsuitable it cannot be done; and the ugly is unsuitable. . . . Therefore, when the carrier of seed approaches the beautiful, he becomes joyful and happy, and he impregnates and reproduces; but when he approaches the ugly, he recoils into himself in pain and sadness, turns back and does not breed, . . . therefore, every soul who wishes to procreate shall follow the beautiful . . . thus, Socrates, she says, Eros does not yearn for the beautiful, as you claim.
>
> But for what?
>
> For breeding and impregnating the beautiful.

Plato, a Darwinist who anticipated Darwin, teaches us that beauty is a guide for successful breeding. Whoever chooses beauty assures favorable descendants, who all inherit the love of beauty. This is how evolution "implants" a trait in the behavior repertoire of a species. A beautiful woman is perhaps the most powerful influence. And who is a beautiful woman? Judith Langlois and Lori Roggman of Texas University give a surprising answer to this question: The beautiful woman is but the average woman, they say. The beauty queen of a certain community, who was chosen for her ability to excite all onlookers, is constructed as a quantitative average of the features of women in that community. For instance, eye size, the distance between them, nose length and width, mouth size and its distance from the chin, face width, forehead span—all are mathematical representations of the average of all women's faces. When many pictures of women's faces were fed into a computer and the computer was instructed to "cook" the average face, hundreds of men and women judged this face to be a more beautiful face than any single face that was input. And the more faces composed the average, so was it judged as more beautiful. The most average is the most beautiful. The average is the definitive epitome of ourselves, and hence its essence of being is "compatible," as the suitable, which assures our continuity—"breeding and impregnating."

The replication mechanisms of genetic matter are equipped with control systems that constantly monitor the compatibility of new combinations. When the mother's DNA matches the father's DNA, replication will succeed; if there is no compatibility, there will be no reproduction. A stallion and mare will produce a promising pony, whereas a stallion and she-ass will make do with a sterile mule. The importance of genetic similarity is covered at length in Chapter 2. The average, for lack of any other information, is the choice with the highest chances for genetic similarity. The average genetic inside as well as the beautiful outside is the supreme approximation of the tribal members to themselves. Those who wish to reproduce successfully will seek the compatible, which is the average, which is the beautiful, which is the correct.

Beauty is in the eyes of the beholder: the she-pig is beautiful to the he-pig, and the average one more so than the exceptional because she assures him descendants, which will enjoy the evolutionary advantages achieved by all pigs so far. The body structure, face, characteristics, personality, and behavior of the average pig constitute the most reliable collection of traits in pigdom, and successful precedents should be repeated.

The fact that a pig is not beautiful in our eyes, but that a mare and deer are is incidental. The fact that one woman is beautiful to Israelis and another woman is beautiful in the eyes of Zulu tribesmen is not incidental: every tribe has a different representative average, and in childhood everyone assimilates the human gestalt of his homeland and is attracted to the beautiful (average) in them.

Evolution has selected in this case, as in many others, a mechanism that combines two elements. One is an inherent basis that can identify predetermined data. For instance, in the case of genetic similarity, a Chinese who grew up in Sweden would be attracted to his own people when he met them even for the first time. Or in the case of compatibility and symmetry, what human being would be attracted to a one-eyed, three-breasted, rat-sized, or elephant-sized mate? This inherent basis is joined by the acquired impressions imprinted in childhood, which become inalienable goods, or wired patterns that would guide the adult's behavior. Just as the female turtle is drawn to lay eggs on the very beach she herself hatched on (this is an imprinted impression assimilated by genetically predetermined brain circuits, which becomes a behavior pattern), so are members of a tribe, a community, and a nation imprinted upon a child's brain, and when one grows up these are beautiful in one's eyes. One's own personal mother, who might have been a redhead, could imprint her appearance and add more value to the rate of beauty attributed to redheads while all factors are weighted.

"Beautiful" is "correct" in more and more areas that were critical enough throughout evolution, so that natural selection has designed judgment and evaluation, attraction and rejection mechanisms for them. For example, a "beautiful view" is one of lush green, clear water, and high peaks, which assure protection and outlook points, all signs of a life-enabling environment. "Paradise" is a tropical rain forest in which our ape forefathers flourished before expulsion. "Hell" is the arid, rocky desert where humans found themselves, when in bartering knowledge for suffering, they descended from the tree tops and learned to walk (upright) on the hostile earth. The opposite is true for the Australian "bearded lizard": the desert is its heart's desire, its habitat of joy. For humans light is a symbol of all that is good and right, and darkness a breeder of the bad and the dangerous. But to the owl, there is nothing better and more promising than the dark. Its aestheticism is upside down. The judgment mechanisms, selected and designed in our brain to enable us to choose correctly; are sensitive to criteria that characterize the correct. We could call them aesthetic criteria. "Aesthetic" could be, for instance, "symmetry": symmetrical limbs are a sign of standardization; monsters are asymmetrical, and no one would want to reproduce in them. Aesthetic might be "harmonious": proportional features, combinations that coexist peacefully. Aesthetic could be "colorful" at the proper time and place: lips should be painted red, eyes, black, and not the other way around, since red lips symbolize a fertile female, healthy and inviting, and black lips symbolize an ill, or perhaps dead, mate.

From the moment accessories expressing the signs of the "correct thing" were selected and built, they became present and active, seeking to show off more and more. In Australia the deep-blue bowerbird flies like a fleeting dream. During the courting season, when he wants to make himself attractive as a mate, the male collects all manner of blue objects—pieces of blue glass, feathers, and shells, and displays them extravagantly as if to say: "Look how blue I am." But the more blueness becomes excessive, the more obliging it becomes. Oscar Wilde used to complain that he found it harder and harder to adapt his lifestyle to his two pieces of blue porcelain. The correct harmony, totally canonical, is a supreme value to the ultimate aesthetician.

The bowerbird is an ancient artist: he takes his initial self and expands it to more and more symbolic blues, and thus enhances his blueness, which is him. Art is a symbolic expansion of ourselves in form, color, symmetry, in a blaze of emotions, senses, thoughts, words, and behavior. Art uses aesthetics as an emotion-evoking tool. Powerful excitement characterizes, to a large extent, the correct behavior in the eyes of evolution. Food and sex, as two prominent examples, are exciting because of their importance to survival. Aesthetics as a judgment and choosing tool is so very important that evolution has made it exciting: the symmetrical, the harmonious, the compatible arouse pleasure and well-being, whereas the dissonant, the anomalous, the exceptional arouse fear, restlessness, and recoiling.

Judgment of beauty, as can be expected from its role in mate selection, distinguishes masculine beauty from feminine beauty. Symmetry is required in both, but size must be differential (he must be bigger than she), hardness must be differential (he is hard, she is soft), color is, to some degree, differential (he is dark, she is fair). Various body proportions are precisely judged. Hip width, waist narrowness, breast size, shoulder strength, chin, beard, eyebrows, body hair—all differentiate feminine beauty form masculine, and we all take pains to look "right" and choose "right." Does the "correct" always necessarily assure fertility and success in raising children? As a somewhat mediocre answer, we can say that at first there was a clear correlation between the correct and evolutionary success. Hip width is indeed essential to maternal ability, but as occasionally happens, evolution drifted to exaggerations, as in the peacock's tail (see Chapter 11).

Beauty attracts us in a powerful way. However, it is not unintentionally that we teach ourselves and our children moral lore, that content should be preferred over shape. Evolution has selected in us an attraction towards intelligent, educated, loyal, kind, bestowing, rich, high-status mates—all characteristics capable of increasing the fitness of our descendants. Beauty turns us on because it signals a merit, and signs of these "content" traits could turn us on too. Morals are yet an additional means to reach the same aim, fortification means. Morals are means that push us to appreciate education, kindness, generosity, status. The basis of the family contract puts the main burden of provision on the father, and accordingly, the aspiration for mates with economic potential was selected in women.

The Israeli kibbutz affords us an opportunity to view the inherent roots of this aspiration. The kibbutz is apparently the only society in the world in which there is no economic dependence of the child on its parents, or of the couple on each other. Every child is assured economic welfare by the community. Every woman enjoys the common standard of living, whether her husband is drunk, ill, in prison, or has deserted her for another woman. And yet, in a study I conducted about kibbutz youngsters' preferences in mate selection, the young girls, just like their sisters all over the world, stressed the importance of economic ability and status in their potential mates (Lampert 1988). Genetic whispers from within are stronger than current knowledge of the socioeconomic culture they were born and live in.

Falling in love, which is ignited when we perceive beauty, that is, when we encounter childhood imprinting, and thus detect a mate who represents the chance to select correctly, was shaped by natural selection in order to make us passionate, to accelerate our enthusiasm for the evolutionary mission. Yet, all over the world, throughout history, we know of cultures, communities, and social groups in which mate selection is dispassionate, disaffected, and coldly calculated. (How could temperature point to a kind of mating, if not because of our deep perception of the connection between cold blood and cold feelings, which was discussed in Chapter 3?) Sometimes mate selection is done by force. Parents force their children to marry mates of their own choice. Sensual excitement is part of the cerebral, neural, and hormonal repertoire of every human, as is the rational, reasoning, and calculating act. A family, or a social group, or a culture could foster some elements of the human possibilities basket, while repressing others. Indeed, every family and every culture does it in one area or another. Young people, who could fall head-over-heels in love, might be obliged to subdue this alternative and marry according to profit-and-gain considerations. Just as in any other talent, the suppression of the ability to fall in love might cause a revolt. These revolts are well known and adorable, and we tell and repeat them again and again. Two of our favorites are Romeo and Juliet, whose very lives were less important to them than their love; and King Edward VIII, whose throne—the ultimate symbol of any possible success—was less important to him than his mighty love for an American divorcee. In terms of cerebral repression mechanisms, we could describe these British dramas, the likes of which can be found anywhere, as guerrilla warfare waged by the excited limbic system against the tyrannical rule of the rational cortex. Falling in love guerrilla stories are favorites all over because the rewards of sensuality are enormous. But dominant rationality actually obeys the same evolutionary criteria: selection of mates, whose advantages will increase the chances of successful offspring.

Surprisingly, marriages that started as cortical calculations are not necessarily worse than marriages that started in limbic passion. Passion slowly dies with time, yielding its place to moderation, habits, partnership, warmth, attention, and mutual aid. The opposite is also true: over time rationality becomes mixed with warm feeling, empathy, concern, mercy, and grace. Our brain is a close-knit fabric of interlacing qualities that foster each other and turn each other on. Evolution, which takes its job seriously, builds a complex network of neural highways, which connect rationality to emotionality, desires to deliberation, eroticism to wisdom, so that optimal functioning is achieved in a human couple's married life over many years. The entrance gate to the network, whether hormonal heat or clear-eyed decision, defines only the beginning of the process, and then all other brain qualities join forces to strive for harmonious, polyphonic, multilayered, many-faceted, long-lasting balance.

15

HOMOSEXUAL LOVE

Throughout this book love has been viewed as an evolutionary product by natural selection based on the close connection between love and reproduction. After all, reproduction is the raison d'etre of natural selection. Homosexual love is seemingly a test case that collapses the entire idea of natural selection for reproduction, for it does not produce offspring. Hence, those who are not happy with the idea of humans and love in biological terms pounce upon homosexual love as if discovering great spoil and use it as evidence that love is not a biological matter.

On the other hand, enthusiasts of evolutionary theories squirm desperately to try and prove the evolutionary advantages of homosexual love. Some, for example, suggest that we should regard homosexual love as a form of altruism between brothers; one brother has children, and the other doesn't but helps the brother raise his. The joint effort is more fruitful than two separate attempts, and thus evolution should indeed select homosexuality.

As is wont to happen with newly founded theories, both sides are somewhat naive and simplistic. First, there might be natural selection of genes which gives an evolutionary advantage (such as a softer man is a better father), yet incorrect dosage or wrong timing, or just a byproduct of the very same advantage—and so they become an evolutionary disadvantage. Second, the process of forming human sexual identity and sexual preferences is a multistage step-by-step process. Genes are only the first step; then comes hormones, tissue, brain structure, and social experiences, and at each of these stages infinite variations are given free rein. A slightly more or slightly less massive brain nucleus, and the personality is different. More than that, any individual human is basically both male and female. Human fetuses, both male and female, indeed carry a pair of sex chromosomes that differentiate the sexes—XX for girls, XY for boys—but for the first six weeks of pregnancy that is all that can tell them apart. Every human fetus has two reproductive systems—ovaries and testicles. A girl can be differentiated from a boy solely by genetic testing. Only after six weeks of pregnancy due to the Testes-Determining Factor antigen (TDF) that is replicated by the Y chromosome, a cascade of processes—genetic, hormonal, and tissue-building and differentiation—cause the twofold sex glands to sort themselves out. With TDF the ovaries degenerate and the testicles grow; when TDF is lacking, the testicles degenerate and the ovaries grow. Sex glands now produce sex hormones. They and only they design sex differences, in both body and brain structure. For six weeks the fetus waits for signals, which will tell it in which direction to develop. Until these signals appear, all are identical; that is to say, all embryos are in a state of dual potential. They are on hold while hormones decide. If masculine hormones appear, a male will develop; if feminine hormones, a female. Dual potential is inherent in all sexual creatures and is realized under well-orchestrated hormonal conductorship. Every one could have been either a man or a woman.

Lizards supply an interesting example. David Crews of Texas brilliantly and meticulously studied a type of lizard called the "whip-tail" that is a modern lizard but still sexless. All the individuals are female; there are no males. The female produces eggs into which she copies entirely her own genetic matter, so that she has a daughter exactly like herself. And yet, these lizards perform all the courting and mating rituals to the letter, as if there were males and females. Who courts and who is courted? Each one courts and is courted according to the monthly cycle. During the first half of the cycle, she acts like a female and is courted; during the second half, she acts like a male and courts. She jumps, mounts, turns to the left, takes two bows to the front, one back, turns to the right with tail between legs, and performs all the intricate steps of the courting dance. How can the same lady be feminine for two weeks and masculine for the next two weeks? Hormones, hormones, hormones.

The hypothalamus is an important brain area for many functions and for sexuality. It has both masculine and feminine centers. One region in the hypothalamus, the ventro-medial-nucleus (VMN), activates feminine behavior, such as offering herself. In another region of the hypothalamus, a few millimeters away, the medial-preoptic-area (MPO) activates masculine behavior, such as mounting (see Figure 9). Both areas exist in every hypothalamus, in every brain, in every creature, male and female. The decision on how to act at a given time is up to the hormones. In embryos, hormones already build stronger tissue on one of the two regions, and then throughout life, they orchestrate behavior by dosage. An affluence of estrogens taken in the feminine area will produce female behavior, whereas an abundance of testosterone in the masculine area will produce male behavior.

Do the "whip-tail" lizards have enough testosterone to act like a male? No. During the second half of the monthly cycle, as all other females do, they have abundant progesterone. Progesterone is surprisingly similar in its chemical configuration to testosterone, and that is what is taken in by the masculine region of the hypothalamus and activates courting behavior. Note carefully that a feminine hormone activates a masculine brain area and produces male behavior in a female!

Is this behavior superfluous, since no sperm has been transferred? No. Courting arouses the courted one in the same way that courting affects a human girl or woman. It increases fertility, and it accelerates the flourishing of the reproductive system. One single mutation, which enabled the reception of progesterone in the hypothalamus's male region, was all that whip-tail lizards needed in order to enjoy the advantages of courting, even with males missing. Simple, yet sophisticated, devices like these are made possible by the fact that every brain holds a twofold sex potential. Both a man and a woman hide in every human.

Figure 9
Sex Differences in the Human Brain

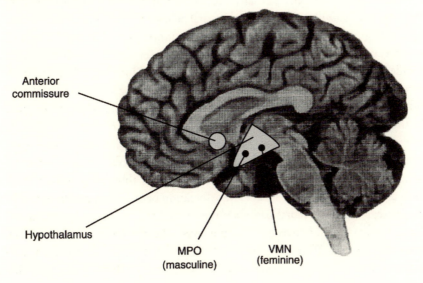

Dual sex potential makes sense when we consider the evolution of sexuality. For most life years on earth, sexuality did not exist at all. Of the 4 billion years, 3 billion were conducted without sex, for better or worse. All individuals of a certain species were identical, and each duplicated itself by using its entire genetic fortune and producing an accurate copy.

When life split into two sexes, evolution moved as minimalistically as always: based on what was before, frugally and prudently, innovations were introduced with the smallest possible investment. A tiny alteration turns two identical creatures into two separate sexes. In diverse types of creatures, this slight change happened differently. In turtles, for example, warmer sun temperature will make females, whereas a drop of five degrees will make males out of the very same eggs. In humans it happens by means of one chromosome out of 46, the puniest and poorest of them all—the Y. But this single chromosome is the outbreak of an enormous cascade of events. Differential sex hormones build diverse, intricate physiological and neural systems, specified to male or female, and thus establish different structural, behavioral, and psychological realities.

Most of the hormonal effect occurs during critical embryonic periods. The fetus is extremely susceptible, and every iota of hormone influences body and brain features forever. This impressionability passes, and it is then much more difficult to affect. Timing is what turns some weeks in a pregnancy into critical periods. Embryos breed adults. Sex hormones are the main designers of human sexuality, and everyone has sex hormones of both kinds, feminine and masculine. Therefore, everybody is both male and female.

The dual potential exists in many animals, and anyone regarding the animals that surround us will easily find homosexual behavior. A cow jumps over a cow, a male dog mounts another male, a bitch mounts a bitch. Highly intensive homosexuality can be seen in one kind of chimpanzee, which lives in Zaire and is called bonobo. In native language bonobo means "little man," due to their great similarity to humans. They might very well be the creatures most like us. When they discover a new cache of tasty food, they become extremely excited. In the height of their excitement, they spend about ten minutes in sexual celebration. Everyone has sex with everyone—male with male, male with female, female with female—and they use every possible variation—face to face, from behind, and so on. After ten minutes of this joyful activity, they calm down and begin their meal. The association between sex and food stems, of course, from the cerebral pathways mentioned in previous chapters, innervating the axial road between the eating area—the amygdala—and the sexual area—the septum. When food ignites their eating area, the sexual area is also activated and the dual potential enables them to calm down in any possible way, heterosexual or homosexual. Frans de Waal, the Dutch researcher who has so thoroughly and affectionately studied the bonobo, describes the wide use they make of sex, also for the purpose of oiling social life. Instead of fighting, competing, and becoming pressured by daily conflicts, they have sexual relations of all kinds and thus make their peace. Females especially succeed in using sex for resolving tension. They broaden the "make love not war" idea to its extreme, and love includes homosexual love, just because it is possible. When we read de Waal's stories and recall the many tensions in our own daily lives, we become envious: if only we would make love, any kind, instead of staying tense, fretful, angry, and resentful.

Humans also have twofold potential, and we could guess that herein lies the reason for discrepancies in various research studies that have tried to estimate the homosexuality rate in the population. Recent U.S. surveys report figures of 2% in men and 1% in women. These are much lower figures than earlier ones. Until recently researchers had agreed on a figure of 10% of the U.S. population. The famous Kinsey Report of the early 1950s cited a figure of 37% of the male U.S. population. The big disparity between 2% and 37% is likely due to the dual potential, by virtue of which many men and women have at least one homosexual experience sometime in their life, and yet still marry and lead normal heterosexual lives. Kinsey's estimate was based on data that included a sometime homosexual experience. On the other hand, a minority of 1 to 2% prefer total homosexuality, and they were measured in the recent surveys.

This distribution in the population, from heterosexuality par excellence through twofold possibilities to homosexuality par excellence, is probably the hormone dosage distribution. A few more or a few less estrogens, a bit more or a bit less testosterone, mainly during the critical embryonic period, may shape adult sexual behavior this way or that way or somewhere in the middle. The critical hormonal influence on the fetus's brain is concerned not only with the constitution of brain areas, but also with ensuing behavioral tendencies, sexual preferences, and the choice of whom to fall in love with.

As an illustration, let us look at a genetic disease called CAH (congenital-adrenal-hyperplasia), in which lack of an enzyme exposes the fetus to more than the normal dosage of testosterone. If it is a male fetus, he will grow up to be very masculine, definitely not homosexual. If it is a female fetus and she was flooded with too much testosterone due to the disease, she will be very masculine throughout her childhood and adulthood. She will be a tomboy, climb trees, play football, and prefer GI Joe to Barbie. She will choose clothes and hairstyles for convenience rather than coquetry. She will favor a "masculine" professional career in technology or engineering, and her probability of being lesbian will rise to 50% compared to 1% of the population. Similar is the story of girls whose mothers took hormonal drugs during pregnancy. Hormonal drugs, whether female progesterones or estrogens, and certainly male testosterones, might affect the fetus in a masculine direction. These girls, although the overdose of hormones was limited to the first term of pregnancy, and their own bodies throughout their entire life spans produce normal feminine dosages, are destined to grow up "masculine" and their chance of becoming lesbians is high.

The variance of hormonal dosage during the critical period of pregnancy can be affected by various factors. There are hereditary-genetic factors such as CAH, which is a genetic disease. There is also a regular variance in the genes' degree of expression. More or fewer hormones, as in any other phenomenon—being tall or short, fat or slim—is a normal variance and not a disease. There are also environmental factors. For example, if a pregnant woman is under stress then the rate of testosterone in her own and her fetus's blood drops. If it is a male baby, this might make him more feminine. The German scientist Gunter Dörner statistically examined the results of stress on mothers of male fetuses in Germany and found that during the Second World War, when mothers were under a lot of stress, three times more homosexual babies were born than before and after the war.

Hormones design the fetus's brain and thus affect the adult's talents, inclinations, and behavior. Those sex regions of the hypothalamus, which in lizards activate male behavior—MPO—or female behavior—VMN—do the same in human brains. As a result of hormonal influence on the fetus's brain, and then for the rest of its life, the masculine area, MPO, contains regions that are, on average, twice as large in men as in women. The American brain researcher, Simon LeVay, consequently found that in homosexual men, as in women, MPO contains nuclei which are two to three times smaller than in heterosexual men.

Another brain area, the anterior commissure, a nerve pathway bunch in the center of the brain, is, on average, bigger in women than in men. The commissure is even bigger in homosexual men than in women. After offsetting men's larger body size in comparison to women's, it was found that the commissure in homosexual men and in women is equal, and is significantly bigger than the average size in heterosexual men (see Figure 9).

These and other areas control sex differences in sexual behavior. Differential levels of sex hormones, mainly during the fetus stage, determine their size and performance in every person. Twofold sexual potential makes possible the emphasis on more feminine areas in men, as well as more masculine areas in women. Variance and distribution around the typical hormonal average of each sex enables an infinite number of variations of masculinity and femininity in every person. There are no two definite sexes, and there is unlimited expanse for hormonal, cerebral, and behavior combinations, in which all humans are distributed.

If the hormonal variance, which forms the variations on the masculinity–femininity theme, were random, then it would be equally distributed in all families. But this is not the homosexuality distribution. Homosexuality tends to appear in some families at higher rates than can be expected from chance distribution. A mixture of a number of studies that examined the frequency of homosexuality by the degree of family closeness reveals data of significant familial tendency. Male homosexuals had 57% identical twins, who were also homosexual, 24% nonidentical twins who were also homosexual, and 13% homosexual brothers. That is to say, the less the genetic closeness, the lower the frequency of homosexual tendency, and yet, it is still higher in a certain family than in the general population. In women there were similar results: 50% identical twins, 16% nonidentical twins, and 13% sisters who were also homosexual.

An examination of familial frequency over the generations points to yet another interesting phenomenon. Homosexuality is transferred mainly by the mother, not the father. How is a hereditary trait transferred by mothers rather than fathers? There are at least two possible hereditary-mechanism candidates for the role. The classic one is chromosome X, which only mothers pass on to male children, while fathers contribute chromosome Y. A group of researchers in the American National Institute of Health, led by Dean Hamer, found, in a first study, a gene on chromosome X which characterized a large part of a group of homosexual men. But this gene's role is unknown, and worse than that, a second study, which repeated the first, refuted its findings. In any case, chromosome X explains maternal heredity in boys but not necessarily in girls, who inherit one X from the mother and one X from the father.

Another possible mechanism consists of the genes on the mitochondrial DNA. Mitochondrion is a small organelle scattered in every human cell whose function is to transform sugar into energy by means of oxidization. Mitochondrion was once a separate organism, assimilated into our ancient single-cell ancestor, and accepted the job of oxidization. Since then, it has been duplicating its DNA independently. This is genetic matter transmitted to offspring only by the ovum, which is a whole cell, and not by spermatozoa, which are only cell nuclei. Thus, every child, male or female, gets its mitochondria only from mother. What do mitochondria genes do? They replicate proteins for various purposes, the most interesting of which for this discussion are enzymes that take part in the synthesis of sex hormones from their raw material, cholesterol. If and when there are mitochondrial DNA mutations, the synthesis and function of sex hormones could change. It seems reasonable to guess that alterations in mothers' mitochondria are behind familial inclinations towards any variance, whether in levels of, or balance between, estrogens and testosterones, and, therefore possibly cause a higher tendency to homosexuality. This guess could perhaps in the future deal with the peculiar phenomena, five to six times stronger than random, that the same mother transfers homosexuality to both her sons and her daughters.

We are getting into deeper water here because simple linear logic would say that sons will be homosexual if exposed to less testosterone, whereas daughters will be homosexual if exposed to too much testosterone, or perhaps, respectively to too many or too few estrogens. How can the same mother's heredity be both too much and too little? Mitochondria, via enzymes, supervise the production of both groups, estrogens and testosterones. Might it be the balance between them, rather than absolute quantities? Perhaps this simplistic thought about more or less testosterones or estrogens is misleading, because brain cells absorb sex hormones largely after they have been converted. Testosterones in men are aromatisized into estrogens; progesterones in women become testosterones.

An additional point of interest is raised by the data that testify to maternal heredity of left-handedness. As suggested in Chapter 5, left-handedness is a result of estrogen–testosterone dosage in the fetus's brain, and is closely associated with speech. It is also related to homosexuality. In a study I conducted, and in other parallel studies, it was found that left-handedness is three times more frequent in lesbians than in the population. In homosexual men, it was also significantly higher than random distribution (Lampert 1994).

Consider the following scenario: a mutation in the mother's mitochondria generated the new dramatic human ability to speak, by means of some estrogenic alteration, perhaps new estrogen receptors in the brain or perhaps a slight change in the estrogen group of hormones to add another member to the old ones, who cannot speak. Right-handedness followed speech. Evolution like both of these human qualities, and so they were selected. From now on, sex hormones influence not only sexuality but also speech and handedness. A variance in estrogen production, or perhaps in estrogen–testosterone balance, which is also mitochondria-dependent, produced both left-handed and homosexual tendencies in a slightly stronger way than dictated by the basic twofold potential in the general population. Mitochondrial mutations are great candidates to explain human speech, if we follow the idea that mothers were behind the urgent need to better understand their helpless kids. If mitochondrial DNA is transmitted only by mothers and its genes affect females in some functions stronger than males, then mitochondrial DNA seems very motherly.

Might not this scenario explain the famous combinations characterizing humankind's great masters of art, like Da Vinci and Michelangelo, both of whom were homosexual and left-handed, with Da Vinci also dyslexic, meaning speech-irregular? I have no answer. Understanding the role of hormones in designing the brain and behavior is still in its infancy. It is my feeling that this understanding will shed light on the design of human sexuality.

Returning now to the debate mentioned at the beginning of this chapter, we do not need to seek an evolutionary advantage in homosexuality, just as we should not cancel its biological context. We can assume that sexuality itself was selected because it affords significant evolutionary value. But the design, the shaping of a human individual's sexuality, is a multistep, complex, and sensitive process. It depends on dosage of various hormones, mainly at the fetal stage. It relies on many factors, genetic and environmental, that can affect the dosage of these hormones, and it is built on the basis of a twofold potential. One is always its own "life story." If a girl has a higher than average level of masculinity and she has experienced rejection from her father, she may become afraid of men and prefer her other side of the dual potentiality and become a lesbian. Another girl whose father also rejected her, was not born with masculine traits and does not prefer women will perhaps stay alone robbed of both alternatives. As a result of the incorporation of all these complicated processes, we get a continuum, or an expanse, of variance on which all humans are set, so that most behave heterosexually, and a minority tend to a greater or lesser degree of homosexuality.

EPILOGUE

Evolution theory has been gaining more and more points in the "explain the world" game, and consequently, more and more ardent followers. Yet many still speak ill of it and condemn it as nothing more than fairy tale. Fortunately, the comparison between evolution theory and fairy tales could be looked upon by goodwill people from the opposite direction, namely, that legendary stories are often an evolutionary reality. A Jewish fable tells the following story: "Our Masters taught: when the sun eclipses it is a bad sign for the whole world. To what can this be compared?—To a king of flesh and blood who offered his slaves a regal feast, and put a lamp in front of them, and then he became angry with them and said to his slave: Take away the lamp and let them sit in the dark." Indeed, this is a fable that is an evolutionary truth. If a solar eclipse took place, the world would go hungry because the world feeds off the sun. There is no life in the dark, for all of life feeds on light.

The sun cascades onto the earth an infinite rain of tiny matter particles called photons, which are light. Life began 4 billion years ago as a process that fed off photons—photosynthesis. The first microorganisms of the evolutionary tale ate light. As long as no one turns off the sun, the evolution of life rolls along: primal life forms accumulate mutations and become more and more complex. The evolutionary modifications accumulated from the first germ to the elephant and to human preeminence, but the basis hasn't changed: a more complex creature eats plants, which eat light. An even more complex creature eats other creatures, which eat plants, which eat light.

Jane Goodall tells the story of Flint, an eight-year-old chimp, who was attached to his mother by strong bonds of love. Young chimpanzees usually grow up close to their mothers for five to six years, and then move on, while she becomes pregnant again. Flint was eight years old and already had a baby brother, but still refused to part from his mother. And she, as is the mother's wont, was compassionate and allowed him to stay close. Then one day a gang fight broke out, and she was mortally wounded. The orphaned Flint got all the possible attention that chimpanzees know how to give orphans. Sisters, aunts, and other kind-hearted ladies brought him food and tried to coax him back to life. But he was inconsolable and refused to eat; he did not respond, retreating more and more into himself, wrapped up in depression. Some days later, he staggered with his remaining strength, laid down under the tree where his mother had died, and breathed his last. Flint died of sorrow, of the loss of love. Mammalian infants drink milk and eat love; Flint died of hunger. Milk is the transfiguration of photons, eaten by plants, which are then eaten by suckling mothers. Love is the transfiguration of photons, eaten by plants, which are eaten by mothers who fondle their children and thus increase their blood levels of growth hormone and insulin and antibodies—all prerequisites of survival. Evolution has made love a prerequisite, without which there is no life. Evolution has turned love into a subcontractor of the sun.

Federico Fellini, the great Italian film director, suffered a stroke some years ago. Julietta Messina, the star of many of his films and his wife, accompanied him on the long struggle after the stroke in an attempt to rehabilitate his life. She tended him hour after hour, day after day, weeks, months, and years, until he suffered a second stroke and died. After his death, Messina lamented that the pipes through which her life had flown for the past 50 years had been severed. She died six months later.

Fellini is preeminent over Flint by an iota. Human preeminence over chimpanzees is in the expansion of love onto more and more objects—not just mother and child, but also man and woman, kin, friends, god, books, art, and even cars. Each and every lover is a subcontractor of the sun. Every lover fondles the other with light, the food of life. Evolution has made every person into a lamp, so that as long as we all go on loving, we will not sit in the dark.

SOURCES AND FURTHER READING

Introduction

Darwin, C. 1877. "A Biographical Sketch of an Infant," *Mind* 2:285–294.

Chapter 1: Love Is Matter

Anonymous. 1970. "Beard Growth," *Nature* 226:869.

Atkins, P. W. 1981. *The Creation*. New York: W. H. Freeman and Co.

Dawkins, R. 1976. *The Selfish Gene*. Oxford: Oxford University Press.

Dawkins, R. 1986. *The Blind Watchmaker*. London: Longmans.

Dennett, D. C. 1991. *Consciousness Explained*. Boston: Little, Brown.

Lampert. A. 1986. "Prolactin in Human Attachment," European Sociobiological Society Conference, Limburg, The Netherlands, presentation.

Nunes, M.C.P., L. G. Sobrinho, C. Calhaz-Jorge, M. A. Santos, J. C. Mauricio, and M.F.F. Sousa. 1980. "Psychosomatic Factors in Patients with Hyperprolactinemia and/or Galactorrhea," *Obstetrics and Gynecology* 55(5):591–595.

Chapter 2: Genes for Love

Bateson, P. 1982. "Preference for Cousins in Japanese Quail," *Nature* 295:236–237.

Hamilton, W. D., R. Axelrod, and R. Tanese. 1990. "Sexual Reproduction as an Adaption to Resist Parasites," *Proceedings of the National Academy of the Sciences* 87:3566–3573.

Manning, J. C., K. E. Wakeland, and K. W. Potts. 1992. "Communal Nesting Patterns in Mice Implicate MHC Genes in Kin Recognition," *Nature 360* (6404):581–583.

Pfenning, W. D., and W. P. Sherman. 1995, June. "Kin Recognition," *Scientific American* 68–73.

Price, J. S. 1995. "The Westmark Trap: A Possible Factor in the Creation of Frankenstein," *Ethology and Sociobiology* 16:349–353.

Pusey, A. E. 1987. "Sex-biased Dispersal and Inbreeding Avoidance in Birds and Mammals," *Trends in Ecology and Evolution* 2:295–299.

Rushton, J. P. 1988. "Genetic Similarity, Mate Choice and Fecundity in Humans," *Ethology and Sociobiology* 9:329–335.

Rushton, J. P., and I. R. Nicholson. 1988. "Genetic Similarity Theory, Intelligence and Human Mate Choice," *Ethology and Sociobiology* 9:45–57.

Russell, R.J.H., P. A. Wells, and J. P. Rushton. 1985. "Evidence for Genetic Similarity Detection in Human Marriages," *Ethology and Sociobiology* 6:183–197.

Shepher, J. 1971. "Mate Selection Among Second Generation Kibbutz Adolescents and Adults: Incest Avoidance and Negative Imprinting," *Archives of Sexual Behavior* 1:293–307.

Weisfeld, E. G., R.J.H. Russell, C. C. Weisfeld, and P. A. Wells. 1992. "Correlators of Satisfaction in British Marriages," *Ethology and Sociobiology* 13:125–145.

Wolf, A. P. 1995. *Sexual Attraction and Childhood Association: A Chinese Brief for Edward Westermarck*. Stanford, Calif.: Stanford University Press.

Chapter 3: The Appearance of Love

Desmond, A. J. 1976. *The Hot-Blooded Dinosaurs: A Revolution in Paleontology*. New York: Dial Press.

Guillette, L. J., Jr., and N. Hotton. 1986. "The Evolution of Mammalian Reproductive Characteristics in Therapsid Reptiles," In *The Ecology and Biology of Mammal-like Reptiles*, N. Hotton, P. D. MacLean, J. J. Roth, and E. C. Roth (eds.). Washington, D.C.: Smithsonian Institute Press, pp. 239–250.

Hofer, M. A. 1984. "Relationships as Regulators: A Psychologic Perspective on Bereavement," *Psychosomatic Medicine* 46:183–195.

Kuhn, C., J. Paul, and S. M. Schanberg. 1990. "Endocrine Responses to Mother–Infant Separation in Developing Rats," *Developmental Psychology* 23:391–399.

Long, C. A. 1969. "The Origin and Evolution of Mammary Glands," *Biological Science* 19:519–523.

McGuire, M. T., and M. J. Raleigh. 1986. "Behavioral and Psychological Correlates of Ostracism," *Ethology and Sociobiology* 7:187–200.

Pond, C. M. 1976. "The Significance of Lactation in the Evolution of Mammals," *Evolution* 31:177–199.

Romer, A. S. 1967. "Major Steps in Vertebrate Evolution," *Science* 158:1629–1637.

Schanberg, S. M., and T. M. Field. 1987. "Sensory Deprivation Stress and Supplemental Stimulation in the Rat Pup and Preterm Human Neonate," *Child Development* 58:1431–1447.

Chapter 4: Maternal Love in Humans

Acsadi, G., and J. Nemeskeri. 1970. *History of Human Life Span and Mortality.* Budapest: Akademiai Kiado.

Coppens, Y. 1994, May. "East-Side Story: The Origin of Humankind," *Scientific American*, pp. 62–69.

Coppens, Y., F. C. Howell, G. L. Isaac, and R.E.F. Leakey (eds.). 1976. *Earliest Man and Environments in the Lake Rudolf Basin.* Chicago: University of Chicago Press.

Eldredge, N., and I. Tattersall. 1982. *The Myths of Human Evolution.* New York: Columbia University Press.

Johanson, D. C. 1996, March. "Face to Face with Lucy's Family," *National Geographic*, pp. 96–117.

Klein, J., N. Takahata, and J. F. Ayala. 1993, December. "MHC Polymorphism and Human Origins," *Scientific American*, pp. 46–51.

Klein, R. 1989. *The Human Career.* Chicago: University of Chicago Press.

Konner, M., and C. Wortman. 1980. "Nursing Frequency, Gonadal Function and Birth Spacing Among !Kung Hunter-Gatherers," *Science* 257:788–791.

Leakey, M. 1995, September. "The Farthest Horizon," *National Geographic*, pp. 38–51.

Leakey, R. E., and R. Lewin. 1977. *Origins.* New York: E. P. Dutton.

Leakey, R. E., and R. Lewin. 1978. *People of the Lake: Mankind and Its Beginning.* New York: Anchor Press.

Leakey, R.E.F., and A. C. Walker. 1976. "Australopithecus, Homo Erectus and the Single Species Hypothesis," *Nature* 261:572–574.

Lee, R. B. 1979. *The !Kung San.* Cambridge: Cambridge University Press.

Lovejoy, C. O. 1974. "The Gait of Australopithecines," *Yearbook of Physical Anthropology* 17:147–161.

Lovejoy, C. O. 1980. "Hominid Origins: The Role of Bipedility," *American Journal of Physical Anthropology* 52:250.

Lovejoy, C. O. 1981. "The Origin of Man," *Science* 211:341–349.

Troyat, H. 1965. *Tolstoy.* Paris: Libraire Artheme Fayard.

Chapter 5: Motherhood Speaks

Bradshaw, J., and L. Rogers. 1993. *The Evolution of Lateral Asymmetries, Language, Tool Use and Intellect.* Sydney: Academic Press, Harcourt Brace Jovanovich, publishers.

Geschwind, N., and A. M. Galaburda (eds.). 1984. *Cerebral Dominance: The Biological Foundation.* Cambridge, Mass.: Harvard University Press.

Kimura, D. 1992, September. "Sex Differences in the Brain," *Scientific American*, pp. 81–87.

Lampert, A. 1994. "Motherhood Language and Handedness" European Sociobiological Society Conference, Krems, Austria, presentation.

Lester, B. M., and C.F.Z. Boukydis (eds.). 1985. *Infant Crying: Theoretical and Research Perspectives*. New York: Plenum Press.

Manning, J. T. 1991. "Sex Differences in Left-Side Infant Holdings: Results from Family Album Photographs," *Ethology and Sociobiology* 12:337–343.

Mellen, L.W.S. 1981. *The Evolution of Love*. Oxford and San Francisco: W. H. Freeman and Co.

Nishida, T. 1993. "Left Nipple Suckling Preference in Wild Chimpanzees," *Ethology and Sociobiology* 14:45–52.

Noirot, E. 1972. "Ultrasounds and Maternal Behavior in Small Rodents," *Developmental Psychobiology* 5:371–387.

Romer, A. S. 1966. *Vertebrate Paleontology*. Chicago: University of Chicago Press.

Salk, L. 1960. "The Effects of the Normal Heartbeat Sound on the Behavior of the Newborn Infant: Implications for Mental Health," *World Mental Health* 12:168–175.

Chapter 6: Maternal Love as a Model

Barth, John. *The Floating Opera*. East Norwalk, CT: Appleton–Century–Crofts, 1956.

Bridges, S. R., R. DiBiase, D. Loundes, and P. Doherty. 1985. "Prolactin Stimulation of Maternal Behavior in Female Rats," *Science* 227:782–784.

Dixon, A. F., and L. George. 1982. "Prolactin and Parental Behavior in a Male New World Primate," *Nature* 299:551–553.

Fava, M., G. A. Fava, R. Kellner, M. T. Buckman, J. Lisansky, E. Serafini, L. Debesi, and I. Mastrogiacomo. 1983. "Psychosomatic Aspects of Hyperprolactinemia," *Psychotherapy and Psychosomatic* 40:257–262.

Frey, W. 1985. *Crying: The Mystery of Tears*. New York: Harper and Row.

Harlow, H. F., and M. K. Harlow. 1962, November. "Social Deprivation in Monkeys," *Scientific American*, 136–146.

Harlow, H. F., M. K. Harlow, R. Dodsworth, and G. Arling. 1966. "Maternal Behavior of Rhesus Monkeys Deprived of Mothering and Peer Associations in Infancy," *Proceedings of the American Philosophical Society* 110:58–69.

Kumar, R., and F. I. Brockington (eds.). 1988. *Motherhood and Mental Illness 2: Causes and Consequences*. Boston: Wright.

MacLean, P. D. 1990. *The Triune Brain in Evolution*. New York: Plenum Press.

Murphy, M., A. Sobol, R. Neff, D. Olivier, and A. Leighton. 1984. "Stability Prevalence," *Archives of General Psychiatry* 41:990–997.

O'Hara, M., J. Schlechte, D. Lewis, and E. Wright. 1991. "Prospective Study of Postpartum Blues. Biologic and Psychologic Factors," *Archives of General Psychiatry* 48:801–806.

Sapolsky, R. M. 1994. *Why Zebras Don't Get Ulcers*. New York: W. H. Freeman and Co.

Chapter 7: Evolution of a Loving Brain

Kling, A. S. 1986. "Neurological Correlates of Social Behavior," *Ethology and Sociobiology* 7:175–186.

Kluver, H. 1959. "The Temporal Lobe Syndrome Produced by Bilateral Ablations," *Ciba Foundation Symposium on the Neurological Basic of Behavior*: 175–182.

MacLean, P. D. 1990. *The Triune Brain in Evolution*. New York: Plenum Press.

Majewska, M. D. 1987. "Action of Steroids on Reward: Role of Personality, Mood, Stress and Disease," *Integrative Psychiatry* 5:258–273.

Rapoport, J. L. 1989, March. "The Biology of Obsessions and Compulsions," *Scientific American*, pp. 63–69.

Reite, M., and T. Field (eds.). 1985. *The Biology of Social Attachment*. New York: Academic.

Wise, S. P., and M. Herkenham. 1982. "Opiate Receptor Distribution in the Cerebral Cortex of the Rhesus Monkey," *Science* 218:387–389.

Chapter 8: The Hierarchy of Love Styles in the Brain

Bernstein, L. 1976, January 7. "Obsessive Ritual By a Performer," *Washington Post*.

Daly, D. 1958. "Ictal Affect," *American Journal of Psychiatry* 115:97–108.

Hediger, H. 1955. *The Psychology and Behavior of Animals in Zoos and Circuses*. London: Butterworth.

Lorenz, K. 1966. *On Aggression*. New York: Harcourt, Brace and World.

MacLean, P. D. 1952. "Some Psychiatric Implications of Physiological Studies on Frontotemporal Portion of Limbic System," *Electroencephalography, Clinical Neurophysiology* 4:407–418.

Osler, W. 1894. *On Chorea and Choreiform Affections*. Philadelphia: Blakiston.

Ploog, D. W., and P. D. MacLean. 1963. "Display of Penile Erection in Squirrel Monkey," *Animal Behavior* 11:32–39.

Williams, D. 1956. "The Structure of Emotions Reflected in Epileptic Experiences," *Brain* 79:29–67.

Chapter 9: The Hierarchy of Sexual Styles in the Brain

Akert, K., R. A. Gruessen, C. N. Woolsey, and D. R. Meyer. 1961. "Kluver-Busy Syndrome in Monkeys with Neocortical Ablations of Temporal Lobe," *Brain* 84:480–498.

Eibel-Eibesfeldt, I. 1971. "!Ko-Buschleute Schwamweisen und Spotten," *Homo* 22:261–266.

Eibel-Eibesfeldt, I. 1989. *Human Ethology.* New York: Aldine de Gruyter.

Gajdusek, D. C. 1970. "Physiological and Psychological Characteristics of Stone Age Man," *Symposium on Biological Basis of Human Behavior,* Engineering and Science 33:26–33, 56–62.

Hite, S. 1974. *Sexual Honesty: By Women for Women.* New York: Warner Paperback Library.

Kitzinger, S. 1984. *Sexualitat im Leben der Frau.* München: Biederstein.

MacLean, P. D. 1964. "Mirror Display in the Squirrel Monkey," *Science* 146:950–952.

Maurus, M., J. Mitra, and D. Ploog. 1965. "Cerebral Representation of the Clitoris in Ovariectomized Squirrel Monkeys," *Experimental Neurology* 13:283–288.

McClintock, M. K. 1971. "Menstrual Synchrony and Suppression," *Nature* 229:244–245.

Prigram, K. H., and M. Bagshaw. 1953. "Further Analysis of the Temporal Lobe Syndrome Utilizing Frontotemporal Ablation," *Journal of Comparative Neurology* 99:347–375.

Robinson, B. W., and M. Mishkin. 1968. "Penile Erection Evoked from Forebrain Structures in Macaca Mulatta," *Archive of Neurology* 19:184–198.

Serafetinides, E. A., and M. A. Falconer. 1962. "The Effects of Temporal Lobectomy in Epileptic Patients with Psychosis," *Journal of Mental Sciences* 108:584–593.

Smith, D. D. 1976. "The Social Content of Pornography," *Journal of Communication* 26:16–24.

Chapter 10: Evolution of Sexuality

Alcock, J. 1989. *Animal Behavior.* Sunderland, Mass.: Sinaver Associates Inc., Publishers.

Bertram, B.C.R. 1975. "Social Factors Influencing Reproduction in Wild Lions," *Journal of Zoology* 177:463–582.

Dawkins, R. 1976. *The Selfish Gene.* Oxford: Oxford University Press.

Fisher, R. A. 1930. *The Genetical Theory of Natural Selection.* Oxford: Clarendon Press.

Fossey, D. 1984. "Infanticide in Mountain Gorillas with Comparative Notes on Chimpanzees," In *Infanticide Comparatives and Evolutionary Perspectives,* G. Hausfater and S. B. Hrdy (eds.). New York: Aldine Press, pp. 217–235.

Hamilton, W. D., R. Axelrod, and R. Tanese. 1990. "Sexual Reproduction as an Adaptation to Resist Parasites," *Proceedings of the National Academy of the Sciences* 87:3566–3573.

Hrdy, S. B. 1974. "Male–Male Competition and Infanticide Among Langurs of Abu Rajasthan," *Folia Primatologica* 22:19–58.

Parker, G. A., R. R. Baker, and G. F. Smith. 1972. "The Origin and Evolution of Gametic Dimorphism and the Male-Female Phenomenon," *Journal of Theoretical Biology*, 36:529–553.

Trivers, R. 1985. *Social Evolution*. Menlo Park, Calif.: Benjamin/Cummings Publishing Co.

Trivers, R. L.. 1972. "Parental Investment and Sexual Selection," In *Sexual Selection and the Descent of man*, B. Campbell (ed.). Chicago: Aldine, pp. 136–179.

Chapter 11: Sexual Strategies

Borgia, G. 1985. "Bower Quality Number of Decorations and Mating Success of Male Satin Bowerbirds: An Experimental Analysis," *Animal Behavior* 33:266–271.

Buss, D. M. 1994. *The Evolution of Desire Strategies of Human Mating*. New York: Basic Books.

Dawkins. R. 1976. *The Selfish Gene*. Oxford: Oxford University Press.

Fitch, M. A., and G. W. Stuart. 1984. "Requirements for a Mixed Reproductive Strategy in Avian Species," *American Naturalist* 124:116–126.

Freedman, D. G. 1979. *Human Sociobiology*. New York: Free Press, Macmillan.

Hunt, M. 1974. *Sexual Behavior in the 1970's*. Chicago: Playboy Press.

Kinsey, A. C., W. B. Pomeroy, and C. E. Martin. 1948. *Sexual Behavior in the Human Male*. Philadelphia and London: W. B. Saunders Co.

Kinsey, A. C., W. B. Pomeroy, C. E. Martin, and P. H. Gebhard. 1953. *Sexual Behavior in the Human Female*. Philadelphia: W. B. Saunders Co.

Le Boeuf, B. J. 1974. "Male–Male Competition and Reproductive Success in Elephant Seals," *American Zoologist* 14, 163–176.

Mealey, L. 1985. "The Relationships Between Social Status and Biological Success: A Case Study of the Mormon Religious Hierarchy," *Ethology and Sociobiology* 6:249–257.

Muscarella, F., and M. R. Cunningham. 1996. "The Evolutionary Significance and Social Perception of Male Pattern Baldness and Facial Hair," *Ethology and Sociobiology* 17:99–117.

Nishida, T. 1990. *The Chimpanzee of the Mahale Mountains, Sexual and Life History Strategies*. Tokyo: Tokyo University Press.

Singh, D. 1993. "Adaptive Significance of Female Physical Attractiveness: Role of Waist to Hip Ratio," *Journal of Personality and Social Psychology* 65:293–307.

Singh, D. 1993. "Body Shape and Women's Attractiveness: The Critical Role of Waist to Hip Ratio," *Human Nature* 4:297–321.

Tooke, W., and L. Camire. 1991. "Patterns of Deception in Intersexual and Intrasexual Mating Strategies," *Ethology and Sociobiology* 12:345–364.

Chapter 12: Long-Term Bonding

Buckle, L., G. G. Gallup, and Z. A. Rodd. 1996. "Marriage as a Reproductive Contract: Patterns of Marriage, Divorce and Remarriage," *Ethology and Sociobiology* 17:373–377.

de Waal, F. 1996. *Good Natured: The Origins of Right and Wrong in Humans and Other Animals*, Harvard University Press.

Diamond, J. 1992. *The Third Chimpanzee*. Jerusalem: Keter Press Enterprises (Hebrew edition).

Goodall, J. 1986. *The Chimpanzees of Gombe*. Cambridge, Mass.: Harvard University Press.

Hausfater, G., and S. Hrdy. 1980. *Infanticide*. New York: Aldine.

Hrdy, S. 1981. *The Woman That Never Evolved*. Cambridge, Mass.: Harvard University Press.

Symons, D. 1979. *The Evolution of Human Sexuality*. New York: Oxford University Press.

Turke, P. W. 1984. "Effects of Ovulatory Concealment and Synchrony on Protohominid Mating Systems and Parental Roles," *Ethology and Sociobiology* 5:33–44.

Wilson, E. O. 1975. *Sociobiology: The New Synthesis*. Cambridge, Mass.: Belknap Press of Harvard University Press.

Wilson, E. O. 1978. *On Human Nature*. Cambridge, Mass.: Harvard University Press.

Chapter 13: Evolution of the Family

Becker, J. B., S. M. Breedlove, and D. Crews. 1992. *Behavioral Endocrinology*. Cambridge, Mass.: MIT Press.

Carter, S. C., and L. L. Getz. 1993, June. "Monogamy and the Prairie Vole," *Scientific American*, pp. 70–76.

Dixon, A. F., and L. George. 1982. "Prolactin and Parental Behavior in a Male New World Primate," *Nature* 299:551–553.

Elwood, R. W., and C. Mason. 1994. "The Couvade and the Onset of Paternal Care: A Biological Perspective," *Ethology and Sociobiology* 15:145–156.

Goodall, J. 1976. "Continuities Between Chimpanzee and Human Behavior," In *Human Origins: Louis Leakey and the East African Evidence*, G. L. Isaac and E. R. McCown (eds.). Menlo Park, Calif.: W. A. Benjamin, pp. 81–95.

Gubernick, D. J., and R. J. Nelson. 1989. "Prolactin and Paternal Behavior in the Biparental California Mouse," *Hormones and Behavior* 23:203–210.

Johanson, D. C. 1996, March. "Face to Face with Lucy's Family," *National Geographic*, pp. 96–117.

Johanson, D. C., and M. A. Edey. 1981. *Lucy, The Beginnings of Humankind*. Tel Aviv: Masada Publishers (Hebrew edition).

Kimura, D. 1992, September. "Sex Differences in the Brain," *Scientific American*, pp. 81–87.

Klein, H. 1991. "Couvade Syndrome: Male Counterpart to Pregnancy," *International Journal of Psychiatry in Medicine* 21:57–69.

Lampert, A. 1998. "Evolutionary Social and Developmental Feminization of the Human Male," In *Research in Biopolitics*, V. Falger, V. D. Dennen and P. Meyer (eds.), JAI Press, forthcoming.

Lipkin, M., and G. S. Lamb. 1982. "The Couvade Syndrome: An Epidemiologic Study," *Annals of Internal Medicine* 96:509–511.

Lovejoy, C. O. 1981. "The Origin of Man," *Science* 211:341–349.

MacLean, P. D. 1985. "Brain Evolution Relating to Family, Play and Separation Call," *Archives of General Psychiatry* 42:405–417.

Myers, D. G., and E. Diener. 1966, May. "The Pursuit of Happiness," *Scientific American*, pp. 54–56.

Rossi, A. S. 1984. "Gender and Parenthood," *American Sociological Review* 49:1–19.

Chapter 14: Mate Selection

Barash, D. 1981. *Sociobiology: The Whisperings Within*. Glasgow: William Collins Sons and Co.

Borgia, G. 1985. "Bower Quality Number of Decorations and Mating Success of Male Satin Bowerbirds: An Experimental Analysis," *Animal Behavior* 33:266–271.

Buss, D. M. 1991. "Do Women Have Evolved Mate Preferences for Men with Resources?" *Ethology and Sociobiology* 12:401–408.

Dissanayak, E. 1992. *Homo Aestheticus: Where Art Comes from and Why*. New York: Free Press.

Heath A. C., and L. J. Eaves, 1985. "Resolving the Effects of Phenotype and Social Background on Mate Selection," *Behavior Genetics* 15:75–90.

Hill, E. M., E. S. Nocks, and L. Gardner. 1987. "Physical Attractiveness: Manipulation by Physique and Status Display," *Ethology and Sociobiology* 8:143–154.

Lampert, A. 1988. "Sex Differences in Mate Selection on the Kibbutz." In *Applied Behavioral Economics*, S. Meitel (ed.), Brighton Sussex: Wheatsheaf Books, pp. 376–385.

Langlois, H. J., and L. A. Roggman. 1990. "Attractive Faces Are Only Average," *Psychological Science* 1:115–121.

Chapter 15: Homosexual Love

Allen, L. S., M. Hines, J. E. Shryne, and R. A. Gorski. 1989. "Two Sexually Dimorphic Cell Groups in the Human Brain," *Journal of Neuroscience* 9:497–506.

Buhrich, N., M. J. Bailey, and N. G. Martin. 1991. "Sexual Orientation, Sexual Identity and Sex Dimorphic Behavior in Male Twins," *Behavior Genetics* 21:75–95.

Crews, D. 1994, January. "Animal Sexuality," *Scientific American*, pp. 96–103.

Crews, D. 1988, May. "Courtship in Unisexual Lizards: A Model for Brain Evolution," *Scientific American*, pp. 72–77.

de Waal, F. 1995, March. "Bonobo Sex and Society," *Scientific American*, pp. 58–64.

Dive, C., T. M. Yoshida, D. J. Simpson, and B. L. Marrone. 1992. "Flow Cytometric Analysis of Steroidogenic Organelles in Differentiating Granulosa Cells," *Biology of Reproduction* 47:520–527.

Dörner, G., B. Schenk, B. Schmiedel, and L. Ahrens. 1983. "Stressful Events in Prenatal Life of Bi- and Homosexual Men," *Experimental and Clinical Endrocrinology* 81:83–87.

Ellis, L., and M. A. Ames. 1987. "Neurohormonal Functioning and Sexual Orientation: A Theory of Homosexuality-Heterosexuality," *Psychological Bulletin* 101:233–258.

Hamer, D. H., Hu, S., V. L. Magnuson, M. Hu, and A. M. Pattatuchi. 1993. "A Linkage Between DNA Markers on the X Chromosome and Male Sexual Orientation," *Science* 261:321–327.

Imperato-McGinley, J., L. Guerrero, T. Gautier, and R. E. Peterson. 1974. "Steroid 5-alpha-reductase Deficiency in Man: An Inherited Form of Male Pseudo-Hermaphroditism," *Science* 186:1213–1215.

Koopman, P., J. Gubbay, N. Vivian, P. Goodfellow, and R. Lovell-Badge. 1991. "Male Development of Chromosomally Female Mice Transgenic for Sry," *Nature* 351:117–121.

Lampert, A. 1994. "Motherhood Language and Handedness," European Sociobiological Society Conference, Krems, Austria, presentation.

LeVay, S. 1993. *The Sexual Brain*. Cambridge, Mass.: MIT Press.

Money, J. 1990. "Androgene Becomes Bisexual in Sexological Theory: Plato to Freud and Neuroscience," *Journal of the American Academy of Psychoanalysis* 18:392–413.

Money, J., and V. G. Lewis. 1987. "Bisexuality Concordant, Heterosexually and Homosexually Discordant: A Matched-Pair Comparison of Male and Female Adrenogenital Syndrome," *Psychiatry* 50:97–111.

Parish, A. R. 1994. "Sex and Food Control in the Uncommon Chimpanzee: How Bonobo Females Overcome a Phylogenetic Legacy of Male Dominance," *Ethology and Sociobiology* 15:157–179.

INDEX

About the Author

ADA LAMPERT is Senior Lecturer in Evolutionary Psychology in the Department of Behavioral Sciences at the Ruppin Institute in Israel. Her research combines the psychology of emotions, sex differences, love, and the family with genetic, hormonal, and evolutionary thinking. Her earlier books have appeared in Hebrew.

Recent Titles in
Human Evolution, Behavior, and Intelligence

Staying Human in the Organization: Our Biological Heritage and the Workplace
J. Gary Bernhard and Kalman Glantz

The End of the Empty Organism: Neurobiology and the Sciences of Human Action
Elliott White

Genes, Brains, and Politics: Self-Selection and Social Life
Elliott White

How Humans Relate: A New Interpersonal Theory
John Birtchnell

Choosing the Right Stuff: The Psychological Selection of Astronauts and
Cosmonauts
Patricia A. Santy

Hormones, Sex, and Society: The Science of Physicology
Helmuth Nyborg

A People That Shall Dwell Alone: Judaism as a Group Evolutionary Strategy
Kevin MacDonald

Dysgenics: Genetic Deterioration in Modern Populations
Richard Lynn

Darwinism, Dominance, and Democracy: The Biological Bases of Authoritarianism
Albert Somit and Steven A. Peterson

Why Race Matters: Race Differences and What They Mean
Michael Levin

ISBN 0-275-95907-4

HARDCOVER BAR CODE